RADIANCE

IF WE ARE THE LIGHT OF THE WORLD,
WHY IS EVERYTHING SO DARK?

RANDY DEAN

DESTINY IMAGE® PUBLISHERS, INC.
P.O. Box 310, Shippensburg, PA 17257-0310

"Speaking to the Purposes of God for This Generation and for the Generations to Come."

This book and all other Destiny Image, Revival Press, MercyPlace, Fresh Bread, Destiny Image Fiction, and Treasure House books are available at Christian bookstores and distributors worldwide.

For a U.S. bookstore nearest you, call 1-800-722-6774.
For more information on foreign distributors, call 717-532-3040.
Reach us on the Internet: www.destinyimage.com.

Trade Paper ISBN: 978-0-7684-3616-7
Hard Cover ISBN: 978-0-7684-3617-4
Large Print ISBN: 978-0-7684-3618-1
E-Book ISBN: 978-0-7684-9048-0

For Worldwide Distribution, Printed in the U.S.A.
1 2 3 4 5 6 7 8 / 14 13 12 11

DEDICATION

I dedicate this book to my amazing wife, Ginger. You have devotedly followed me through more than a dozen moves, including one that took you from your beloved native country, Texas. You've never flinched nor complained, because you love from a depth of character and purity that few humans possess, much less enjoy. You are the Radiance of Him to me. Thank you.

Acknowledgments

Bill Johnson, pastor of Bethel Church in Redding, California, is rapidly "owning" my heart as an apostolic father. His influence can be seen throughout this book.

Bill Johnson's senior associate, Kris Vallotton, kicks my spiritual behind routinely, and his influence is woven herein as well.

Pastor Dan and Sheila Rhodes of Atlanta, Georgia… why does the sound of these names make me smile? Because friendships like ours are transcendent.

My daughter, Libby, and son, Jonathan, who love me and through that love put a demand on my heart; when your children want you to be their pastor you have no choice but to give your best.

My son-in-law, Darren, who makes me want to walk on water and would rescue me if I sank.

My daughter-in-law, Abby, whose trust compels me to be real.

Eden, Ayla, and Asher, our astonishingly brilliant grandchildren, have become a whole new kind of motivation to impart to an entire generation the freedom to be radiant with a Transcendent Supremacy, unencumbered with previous generations' religious baggage.

My spiritual sons and daughters at Living Word Chapel—20 years of Kingdom living together has created a radiance on that frozen hill.

There are many others whose names you will read in the chapters that follow. Some of those names I have intentionally held from this spot to give you a chance to at least start reading the book before making any judgments that might otherwise prevent you from getting past the first dozen pages.

ENDORSEMENTS

What is the value of my long-term friendship with Randy Dean and his family? Incalculable! In over 25 years we've faced incredible joys and sorrows of life together… both humanly and ecclesiastically. For years we've arched off one another's revelation of the Kingdom of God. However, after reading his book, I see more than a dear friend; I see the power of God exploding out of his heart into the hearts of all his readers…including mine!

Randy's sheer passion for God and His supernatural work in human life is irresistible. If it sounds like Randy may be on the edge…it's because he *is*! He's on the cutting edge of shocking Christians out of mediocrity and challenging them to be who God destined them to be. What a concept! Randy isn't just teaching you about God's Kingdom; he's describing it from his fervent perspective of being totally consumed by it! He's not preaching transcendent presence; he's passionately living in the midst of it! He's not just telling about Jesus; he's introducing you to his closest friend!

Let there be no doubt about it. Randy Dean is a shepherd…even a shepherd's shepherd. His heart beats in rhythm with the Great Shepherd. He walks daily with

God's people, weeps with them and over them, as he leads them into green pastures. But beware, dear reader, Randy's dry and sometimes pithy humor drives his point home well. He doesn't spare any of our sacred cows; he sacrifices them all on the altar of the person of Jesus. He shakes us from our religious concepts and traditional clichés that many of us have blindly accepted. However, his book does more than rev up our spiritual motors; it gives us ways to demonstrate God's love to the world that desperately needs to see the real Jesus...not a religious one. His masterful flow of words apprehends more than our imaginations; they arrest our very spirit and soul and lead us to God Himself.

Randy, your exhilarating persuasion draws people into the realm of the impossible! Write on, my friend! The Church and the world need to hear God's heart through you.

Dan Rhodes
Founder, Destiny Navigators
www.destinynavigators.org

If you are looking for a book on theology, then keep looking (I can make some good suggestions!). However, if you are looking for a book that will grab you by your spiritual throat and shake you into action beyond yourself, then by all means read Pastor Randy Dean's *Radiance*. While it is not a book on theology, it is certainly a theological book—chock-full of Scripture references and biblical insights—but what it suggests (no, what it *insists* on) is that believers not be lulled into complacency by weak-hearted, short-sighted religion, but instead embrace the life-changing, world-changing reality of the Kingdom of God, which was the message that radiated from the heart of Jesus and the apostles.

Reading this book left me challenged and convicted, and also left me shouting "Amen!" to the propositions Pastor Randy presented. In short, what would happen if Christians actually believed and acted on the things Jesus declared? We would change, people around us would change, and we would radiate the very glory of God that dwells in us. Things would start to happen. If the message of this book is embraced, things *will* start to happen. Jesus said, "Heal the sick, cleanse the leper, raise the dead, cast out demons" (see Matt. 10:8). How about we actually *do* this for a change?

Bishop Kenneth Myers
Pastor, Christ's Church Cathedral
Sherman, Texas
Author of *The Garden of Happiness* and
What Christians Believe

Upon reading Radiance, an awakening of God's power has enveloped and drawn me deeper into the very heart of His presence. Pastor Randy Dean's powerfully anointed book has opened my spirit eyes to a deeper understanding of the supernatural and the quality of life Jesus desires for all of us to live and walk in. It is the timing for God's Transcendent Radiance to be imparted to a broken and hurting world. We, as Christ's Bride, are called to be a healing and a solution to their brokenness. The undeniable passion in which Pastor Randy has written this book is instantly contagious. It is the heart of God crying out to a people for His Holy Spirit radiance to be a consuming fire with unlimited power. This power will make a difference in the world in which we live so others will see His glory, potential, and radiance in us. Let His radiance consume us as we run toward it!

Sheila D. Rhodes, Pastor's Wife
(Pastor Dan Rhodes)
and Dear Friend to the
Dean Family for more than 25 years

The Lord said, "Whom shall I send? And who will go for us?" Randy Dean said, "I will! Send me!" And so you have this fiery, passionate gift of a book in your hands.

Reading Radiance is grappling with the Holy Spirit, at full blast, through a fire hose! It will bring you to your knees; it did me! The book demands a response. Not a "response" of interminable consideration or eternal pondering. It demands action: either open your life entirely to knowing God and experiencing His profound love, His transforming radiance (and strap in for the ride of your life!), or resist and live that to which you've grown accustomed. Embrace the former and the promise and power are Kingdom Come to Earth. Continue in the latter and nothing changes, not you or anything within your influence. Do not read this book if you want to remain the same!

Shaun R. Floerke
Duluth, Minnesota

TABLE OF CONTENTS

PREFACE

I have intentionally tried to keep printed quotes from the Bible to a minimum in this book. Only where I felt it absolutely imperative have I included more than a line or two from any particular verse. Why? Because I want readers to open the Bible in the version of their choice (mine is the New American Standard...you have it your way, I'll have it the right way!) and look at the verses with their own eyes and with the entirety of a passage or story available for their own view.

There are also a few places where I have intentionally left out the specific address for a Bible reference. It is my hope that the reader will do his or her own investigation. Anything I can do to get people to turn the pages and pour over The Book, I will do. Sometimes I will give you the address of the Scripture I'm referring to; sometimes I won't. There won't be a particular pattern to this other than my cheerful whim. Either way I will leave it for you to search out the details and the surrounding landscape of the passages. I have not hidden them from you; I have left them hidden for you. Happy hunting.

For the sake of confidentiality, I have changed some names. Also, I have been careful to occasionally alter story details for the sake of privacy while remaining true to the outcomes. No core truths, my integrity, or animals have been injured in the making of this book.

Introduction

According to Hebrews 1:1-3, God sent Jesus as His Radiance. The word translated as "radiance" here has the meaning of a breaking out of light, a sunrise and daybreak....

I'm sitting by a window with the sunrise directly in my face. It's a brittle, cold, 4 degrees Fahrenheit Wisconsin morning, and that sunlight seems to be saying, "Hey, winter! You act all big and bad right now, but I'll just keep breaking out up here, day in and day out. I will influence you. It's just a matter of time. Your icy grip is temporary. My flames are not."

That's exactly who Jesus is.

Habakkuk 3:4 says, *"His radiance is like the sunlight; He has rays flashing from His hand...."* Little wonder, then, that when Jesus touches people, they are healed. Little wonder, then, that we are commanded to lay hands on the sick.

Isaiah 60:1-5 starts with one of the best known verses in the Bible that also holds a promise of radiance. The prophet tells us to arise and shine for our light has come and the glory of the Lord has risen upon us. The result is that we will be "radiant." I love this—He is the glory behind the potential of our radiance.

Then there is Moses who comes down from the mountain with his face shining, *"because of his* [Moses] *speaking with Him."* Need more? Second Corinthians 3:7-18 says that the glory of Moses' facial shine is nothing in comparison to what the Spirit of God intends to be and do in and through us.

"Now wait a minute," you may be saying. "You aren't suggesting that we should seek a 'glow' or an 'aura' are you?" No, I am not suggesting that at all. I am positively shouting for us to explode out of what is normal, routine, safe, vanilla, customary, harmless, typical, standard, predictable, and dim!

"Arise and shine" means that when and if we arise, we will shine! It is only in the arising that there will be a shining.

Today's Western version of Christianity is losing a battle we were otherwise destined to win. People flounder in darkness, breaking their toes on every sidewalk crack. Yet all too often our reply has been, "Alas, if only they would open their eyes…poor little darklings…." This reply is totally unacceptable, especially in the view of such promises as I have just presented and will continue to press throughout this book.

What surrounds Jesus is The Radiance. Come into that vortex and you will change. The more quality exposure to this heat that you allocate yourself, the more you allow its inherent transcendence to automatically melt winter into the transfiguration of spring.

Think about that. Right now, the rays of sunlight hitting my face through this eastern window came from outer space, traveling here at 186,000 miles per second. At its source, the sun's surface, the heat of the sun's radiance is approximately 12,000 degrees Fahrenheit (some astronomers estimate the core of the sun is 36,000,000 degrees Fahrenheit). The sun is 93 million miles from earth, and it took 500 seconds for that sunbeam to get here.

Upon its arrival on my face, it is perfect warmth.

Malachi 4:2 says that there is healing in His "wings." Here again, the inference in this passage has to do with the rays of light, like wings, shooting off the sun. Carry that Radiance with you and your surroundings are profoundly impacted. Enhance that Radiance through faith, prayer, and, most importantly, intimate covenant relationship, and a neighborhood, a region, a state, and a nation are ultimately healed. God's goal, which should be ours, is that the whole earth is changed under the Radiance of this Transcendent Supremacy.

The authentically Good News of the Kingdom of God is a transcendent, living energy that by its sheer magnetism draws people into its healing force. It is more than a teaching, more than a doctrine, and most certainly much more than a complicated dogma about the endtimes.

You'll see that word, *transcendent*, and its variations many times throughout this work. If it starts to sound repetitious, good; that means you are paying attention. *The use of a word with complete intentionality can forge new pathways of thought. If the pathway is clear enough, a new lifestyle can begin.*

A brief look at the dictionary tells us that *transcendent* means to surpass, pass beyond, and to exceed. In theology it is used to express that which exists beyond the material, created universe. The supernatural.

The last two popes have talked a great deal about a restoration of transcendence to Christianity. Eastern Orthodox theology speaks of the "uncreated light" that dwells in us as rooted in the transcendence of God. Poets and artists reach for it routinely. I'm convinced that while the specific word is not used in Scripture, it is most certainly found on almost every page. "A force of the immaterial" is a new phrase I like to use to describe it.

Our material world came from "there." When you take transcendence out of the Scriptures, you're left with little more than a table of contents and the maps. Even the Ten Commandments came from "there." And "there" is defined by Jesus as "the Kingdom of God."

I am fond of saying that the Kingdom of God is a Transcendent Supremacy. It knows no other way to be but superior to all other realities. Remember the sun shining in my face?

Why else would Jesus say in Luke 16:16 that the Kingdom of God had such transcendent influence that simply in the words of it, that just by its announcement, "everyone" was forcing their way into it?! What would that look like today? And where has this force of the immaterial gone?

To find the answer I've combed through the lives and works of some notable and some less-known Kingdom believers. Recently I found a treasure in the words of E. Stanley Jones in his landmark book, *The Unshakeable Kingdom and The Unchanging Person*:

> But when we lose the Kingdom, as Christendom has in large measure, then our very light turns to darkness. The relativisms to which we turn don't relate; our half-answers don't answer; the props upon which we lean break and pierce our hands and our hearts with disappointment; our goals recede for we are not on the Way. Our light has turned to darkness. "If therefore the light that is in thee be darkness—how great is that darkness." Even the doctrine of the Kingdom can become darkness if it remains a doctrine. A leading theologian said, "I'm tired of the doctrine of the Kingdom," and it was to him largely a doctrine, a doctrine instead of a direction. When we bind up the Kingdom and Parousia, the Second Coming, our light has turned to darkness, for Jesus, when He was here, went about preaching the gospel of the Kingdom. It is at your doors, has come upon

you, it is within you, you enter it now by being born again—now—by being converted—now. It was the program for life now. You seek it first and all these will be added to you, now. To tie up the Kingdom of God with His Second Coming is without warrant. To say we can do little or nothing until He comes is to have our light turn to darkness. The Kingdom of God is God's total answer to man's total need now. It is a total program for man's total life now.[1]

All too often we have preached the Good News *about* Jesus. On the other hand, Jesus came announcing the Good News *of* the Kingdom of God. It's the difference of the Good News *about* and the Good News *of*.

Jesus didn't land on the shores of earth proclaiming Himself, even as great as He was. Nor did He say, "Hey everybody! I'm here! My name is Jesus and I'm preaching the Good News of, well, Jesus! Just say the sinner's prayer and conclude it by sincerely saying My name…so that when you die you'll go to Heaven. Oh, and here's an extra bonus. Someday, and only if you're really good boys and girls, when My Father and I have really had it with the bad people, we'll rapture you up and out before we roast the planet."

Sorry about that. I should only open one can of worms at a time.

What He *did* do was announce the very real influence of being the King of His Kingdom—the really good news of a Transcendent Supremacy that is right at your hand waiting for your grasping hunger to make it the grand adventure and tangible reality of your life. We have been called to be the bearers of an insuperable sovercignty!

Yes, we too are potentially radiant with a Spirit World of an invulnerable, irresistible, and pervasive force. When we learn to touch the world with that Transcendent Supremacy, we will see the dead raised, the blind now seeing, and the lame walking! (See Matthew 10:7-8.)

I am quite serious about this. I don't think the Gospels can be read any other way except to see and know that Jesus was the bearer of an invulnerable, irresistible, and pervasive force. This is the quality of life He introduced, and this is how He would like for us to live. I pray that the pages of this book will draw you to an inescapable desire for His Life in yours.

While I am grateful that Jesus gave us eternal life in Heaven after we die, I have come to an inescapable revelation of His Kingdom and His Life: *Eternity is a quality of life more than a quantity of incalculable years.*

It is that quality, that transcendence, and Kingdom that I want to explore with you through these pages. I've been pounding these words into my computer for two and a half years, but in truth, I've been incubating them and passionately seeking to live them throughout 35 years of ministry. These are my passionate ponderings. I may not be the only one saying these things, but I am one. I pray

they will contribute, in ways small or great, to a reforma-
tion and a new American Awakening.

ENDNOTE

1. E. Stanley Jones, *The Unshakeable Kingdom and
   The Unchanging Person* (Abingdon Press, 1972),
   189.

Chapter 1

"If Offended You Must Be..."

I do not seek to offend you;
but if offended you must be,
then I am your man.
—Ern Baxter

I have long ago stopped trying to terrify people with "going to hell." You can't scare people who are already living there, whether they admit it is hell or not. Someone once said, "Religion is for people afraid of going to hell. Spirituality is for people who have already been there." I would add, religion seems to *need* the threat of hell far too much. So, I've changed my challenge.

I remember "evangelistic" meetings that used to close with the piano playing softly and the preacher intoning, "All heads are bowed and every eye is closed. Eternity is standing before you this night. If you walked out of this church tonight, drove down the road and a drunk driver crossed the yellow line and hit your car, head-on (there are several variants to this proposal such as: getting run over by a truck, train, or other enormous vehicles), do you know where you will spend eternity?"

I can no longer endorse the above approach. I've simply found a more excellent way. With the perfect beauty of Christ and the truly amazing grace of the Father at my disposal I refuse to wave hell in the face of people who have already spent too much time living there.

These days I look church gatherings in their collective eye and say, "With everyone looking and everyone as honest as you know how to be, if by some stroke of God's grace and love you should leave here today and *live* for any number of additional days or years, will you be living Heaven or hell on earth? Because, frankly…*where you are is where you're going.*"

Where you are is where you are going. If where you are is healthy, then where you are going is healed. If where you are is Heaven, then Heaven is already your home. If where you are is hell, then God is offering you a new address, today.

On the eyes open or closed matter, I've got to chase a rabbit trail for just a moment. I cannot ask people one minute to close their eyes and raise their hands, implying privacy, and then the next minute ask those same people who had a moment of privacy to come forward publicly. For me, that's too close to "bait and switch." Maybe it's just splitting a hair and maybe there are thousands of you shouting back at this page telling me how it worked for you. I'm only saying I can't do that.

Back to the point. For the life of me, I don't see Jesus' ministry as one that perpetually addressed, "If you were to die tonight…where would you go?"

I do know that Jesus said, *And everyone who lives and believes in Me will never die…"* (John 11:26). But I also know that the transcendences of the Kingdom of God implore me to dive more deeply into the Life of that Word. There are two words here that deserve more attention: *"never die."* How would you respond to someone who looked you squarely in the eye and said, "Everyone who lives and believes in me shall never die"?

Never die?

Notice that in the context of the aforementioned passage, Jesus dropped that bomb of Truth in the sensitive moment of a grieving sibling's complaint of His late arrival to *prevent* a death. Did He give any more information on the spot to clarify what He really meant, which for many of us, is safely and simplistically filtered down to, "When you die you will go to Heaven"? No!

In fact, He identified Life and Resurrection as being *Himself* right there on the spot. Not a concept, not a decision card we sign…but *Him.* Life and Resurrection is standing there on two feet, blinking His eyes and speaking. To be perfectly honest with you, if I had been standing there,

I would have asked, "So, Mr. Life and Resurrection. Can I touch You?"

What's more, He followed this shocking comment by successfully calling a man out of his tomb. Is it just me, or does that add something a bit more intriguing to the whole matter? It seems to me that the act of calling a man out of the grave implied a bigger proposition than, "When you die you will go to Heaven."

Again, if I had been on that scene, I know I would have come away from that entire series of events with far more on my mind than, "If I get hit by a bus tonight, will I go to Heaven or hell?"

In fact, the act of Jesus raising Lazarus from the dead implied *and* imposed on the moment the power of the good news of the presence of the Kingdom of God in the person of Jesus Christ. A Transcendent Supremacy had arrived and the nature of this Kingdom is unrivaled prominence, even over death. It does not come to share a space. It comes to pervasively take over whatever ground it touches. That's what I mean by a Transcendent Supremacy that's just within hand's reach.

The conversation preceding Lazarus' resuscitation underscores this point. When Jesus assures Martha with, "Your brother shall rise again," she answers with the standard religious fare, "I know he will rise again in the resurrection on the last day." You can't completely blame her for that, but it does beg the question: How much of what Jesus is offering us today have we all assigned to the *last day* that very well may be looking us in the eye for *this day*?

While we're busy making doctrinal statements, Jesus would like to make a living resurrection statement.

I'll take this one step further. I approach all of God's Word and Ways with a wide-ranging but single-eyed question: How does this live, breathe, bleed, and then come alive from the dead? Theological accuracy, for me, flows out of the Word made flesh in the living, breathing, bleeding, and resurrected paradigm in the Life of Jesus Christ.

"What is Truth?" is a shallow imitation for the appropriate question: "*Who* is Truth?"

I am no longer obligated to study Truth. Now that I have a passionate love relationship with Truth, my study grows out of the complexities of that camaraderie.

He lived and breathed, and the Word lived and breathed. He bled and died, and the Word bled and died. After three days in the tomb, the Word was resurrected and now the Word is exalted *in Him.* I come to a Transcendent Supremacy when I come to this Word, and this Word is The Word of the Kingdom of God.

Other books, ministries, and people smarter than I am can debate all they want in defending their doctrines, thumping their knowledgeable chests! I just want to know how Truth lives, how Truth breathes, and, ultimately, how Truth bleeds and then climbs out of the grave to live invulnerably! The message of the Kingdom of God in the life, person, and presence of Jesus Christ takes me there.

Bill Johnson, senior pastor of Bethel Church in Redding, California, says it this way: "Only Jesus is perfect theology."

Jesus did not come to start a new religion. He did not come to take sides politically. He came to take over! His Kingdom is what He is all about. Jesus' proposal to us about His Kingdom is so expansive, so all encompassing, that He promised if we seek the Kingdom first (to aim at, strive for it in all our pursuits), then every need of our lives will be met.

Read the Sermon on the Mount in Matthew 5, 6, and 7; it is the Constitution of King Jesus and His Kingdom. No religious trappings, no religious bigotry, and no religious heavy-handedness here. We are to think of birds and grass and flowers as the basis of our life and living. Forget about religious appearances; think perfume, fish, and trees. And when it comes to the art of "preaching" (a personal favorite of mine), think of a Transcendent Authority that bounces the heads of religious power brokers, stymies dark forces, and frees people with a breath.

Read Matthew 13 as if you have never seen or heard of it before. The parable of the sower and the seed is all about the Word of the Kingdom. It's the Word of the Kingdom that prophets and the righteous have desired to see and hear. It's the Word of the Kingdom that terrifies the evil one so much that he labors long to steal it away from its transcendent potential. The evil one knows that it is the Word of the Kingdom that *must* bring forth a hundredfold increase! It's the Word of the Kingdom that will grow until it is larger than any other plant in the garden. The evil one cannot rest with that kind of transcendent Seed lying in the ground. It threatens his very existence.

Kill or slander the sower of the Seed, but you cannot escape the power of the Seed sown. It is an insuperable sovereignty packed with the DNA of Heaven poised for an explosion of Transcendent Life from a world waiting in the wings.

Bear with me, please. I'm taking aim at something beyond even what I just said. Up to this point everything in this chapter is a foundation for what comes next. Follow me closely.

This book is the product of 35 years of pastoral ministry, most of which has been rooted in passionately calling people to live and breathe in the Kingdom of God, not as a plane ticket to get "over yonder," but as power to overcome in the down and dirty here and now. Note that I said, "most of which."

Early on I struggled mightily with the sense that what I believed and what I desperately tried to preach with passion just dribbled out of my mouth and drooled off my chin and dripped onto my shirt.

I read about the heroes of the faith who died for what they preached. Me? I was just dying after I preached because the sermon I just finished was painfully shallow and I knew it.

I admired Martin Luther King Jr., for instance, and loved his writings, sermons, and speeches. But I could not help but notice two little things: his message *lived* and *breathed* in a way that stunned the world, and his message was ultimately signed in his own blood. Now his message and dream are alive from the grave and live invulnerably. That's a Transcendent Supremacy; that's a force of the immaterial; *that's the Kingdom of God.*

In 1984 my wife and I were at a spiritual impasse. What I just described was eating away at me. I was tired of trying to emulate passion with the end result just being the drool on my shirt. We went on an extended fast to clear the spiritual air around us and reach for the answers we needed. Thirty-eight days into our fast God gave us the "all clear," time to eat. At the time, I mentioned to God that in two more days we would be at the 40-day mark. I'll never forget His answer: "No…if you go 40 days it'll ruin everything. You will be caught up in pride and I'll have to break that. Your heart is right, for now. Go ahead and eat." In retrospect, this was the perfect answer for us.

Out of that fast and through a series of distinctly divinely-ordered events, God put a spiritual father in our lives (see 1 Cor. 4:15). We didn't even know to ask for a spiritual father or what to call it in those days. We didn't know how important this truth would be to us down through the decades to come.

We just knew that God had unmistakably stamped into our lives a man of God whose fathering spirit revealed the living, breathing, bleeding, and resurrected message of the Kingdom of God.

We've learned since to appreciate what the apostle Paul meant when he told people to "imitate" him. I take this to mean that if you looked deeply enough in his eyes you would eventually see Christ looking back at you through those apostolic eyes.

To be completely honest, however, this spiritual father shocked me at first. I had to get past my own internal dialogue/argument thing with his messages when I started listening to his teaching, but the shock jolted me out of my *narrow-see* (rhymes with *Pharisee*) vision.

You know what I mean by the internal dialogue/argument thing, don't you? God calls it "gainsaying" or being "obstinate" (see Rom. 10:21). It means to maintain a running argument in your mind, in which, of course, you always "win," or better put, one side of you wins, not knowing that what you are losing is the potential of a renewed mind.

Some of you reading this may be doing that right now. Fighting me, answering my propositions—and you probably will throughout this book—that is, if you make it past these paragraphs, or if you make it past the following affirmation.

Ready? Let me gavel this meeting to order and ask for your complete attention.

Chapter 2

"Offend Your Mind to Find Your Heart"

God will often offend your mind
to find your heart.
—Bishop Earl Paulk

B ishop Earl Paulk from the Cathedral of the Holy Spirit in Atlanta, Georgia, is the man I was referring to in the previous paragraphs who became my spiritual father. Some of you know that name, some of you don't. Facts and rumors about him have become welded together so much so that hardly anyone, perhaps not even he himself, knows what's real and what's been made up. The realities are tough enough to navigate, much less the rumors.

All I know for certain is that without his courage to break the Bread of Life in the message of the Kingdom of God back in the 1980s, I would still be stuck, along with many in the Body of Christ, where I was. I will never forget how he bravely called us forward in the first series of messages I heard him preach: "The Wounded Body of Christ."

Some people would argue that I've now cursed this book by acknowledging the bishop by name. I would argue that I would have cursed it by failing to honor his role in my life. Our relationship, once functional, treasured, and productive, has changed dramatically.

I have recently moved my life, family, ministry, and church into a beautifully functional apostolic covering with Rich Oliver and The River, Bill Johnson and Global Legacy. That being said, I will always acknowledge that Bishop Earl Paulk was a man sent from God to open my eyes and the eyes of millions to the rich revelation of the Kingdom of God, NOW.

Yes, I know what some of you believe about this man and I also know what the realities are, good, bad, and everything in between. As I said a moment ago, rumor phases back and forth into and out of truth, so much so that my heart aches at *every* level, fact, fiction, and rumor, for what has become the reality surrounding this once thundering warrior for the Kingdom of God.

Remember how I said that I just want to know how Truth lives, how Truth breathes, and, ultimately, how the Truth bleeds and then climbs out of the grave to live invulnerably?

That is why I stand in the middle of what has become for me, the bloodied words of Paul, *"For if you were to have countless tutors in Christ, yet you would not have many fathers…"* (1 Cor. 4:15). And the bloodied words of Malachi 4:6, *"He* [the spirit of the prophet Elijah] *will restore the hearts of the fathers to their children, and the hearts of the children to their fathers, so that I will not come and smite the land with a curse."*

And, again, the bloodied, living words of Paul, Moses, and Solomon that tell us that honoring parents is the commandment with promise and that binding their teaching to our hearts will guide us, cover us, and continually enlighten us (see Eph. 6:1-3; Exod. 20:12; Prov. 6:20-23).

I know well the effect these words can have on certain schools of church folks. You might call them the Bible Fish. When met head-on with matters that offend their sensibilities, their mouth forms a perfect circle, their eyes open wide, they grab their Bibles, and they grow fins. They dive into the scriptural pool of only what they know and they start desperately flipping through the pages attempting to protect their own mind against the possibility of any revealed mental health getting through and producing a renewed mind.

Once again, and for the record, let me hasten to say that I know the scandals, the hearsay, the fabrications, and *yes*, I know the painful truths. Yet, I know much more deeply than all of these that God profoundly and unmistakably put this man in my life as a spiritual father who planted in me the revelation of the Kingdom of God.

Where would Solomon be if he had decided to un-father David for the great scandal that ultimately sired him? Once we remove the rose-tinted glasses from our eyes and read the Bible for its reality, we are forced to accept some mysteries, which forge realities beyond our frail sensibilities.

Consider the texture of the stories surrounding the two most celebrated figures and stories of the Old Testament:

Moses was a fugitive murderer who was never brought to justice, who never, that we know of, publicly repented, and yet he boldly proclaimed God's commandment, *"You shall not murder"* (Exod. 20:13). While some folks said to Moses, *"You exalt yourself above the assembly"* (Num. 16:1-33), God clearly had an entirely different opinion of His man. Revelation upon revelation and multiple dynamic encounters with God that can hardly be fathomed followed Moses all the days of his life. Yet, he wouldn't make it past my own church's background check to assist in our nursery today.

Saul feared the opinions of people and God rejected him as King of Israel; David feared God alone. So much so that Jesus fearlessly testifies of His lineage, *"...I am the root and the descendant of David..."* (Rev. 22:16). In a manner of speaking, isn't Jesus saying that David is a spiritual father by calling Himself "descendant" or "offspring"?

Didn't Jesus realize the potential of hurting His reputation, not to mention His book sales, by tagging the end of the Bible with that reference? After all, didn't David do that whole nasty deed with Bathsheba? And later, when he learned that he had gotten Bathsheba pregnant, didn't he call her husband in from a war front and try to set him up to have a date with his wife to cover his own stupid deed?

Then, when her husband, Uriah, could not bring himself to enjoy a romantic night with his wife lest he dishonor the sacrifices of his army and his nation, didn't David get the guy drunk in order to trick him into having sex with his wife? *Yikes!* Can this cesspool smell any worse?

And then, when that failed, didn't David write orders to have Uriah sent to the bloodiest battle front, and gave that same death warrant *to* Uriah to take to his superior officer? Isn't it a verified historical account that David started this whole ugly mess by being a peeping tom? Without a doubt the answer is yes to all of the above, and yet Jesus is not afraid to call Himself the offspring of David.

Of course, I know that this isn't the end of the story for David. As of this writing, what you and I *don't know* is the end of the story for Bishop Earl Paulk. Maybe it gets worse, maybe it gets better, but the point is, *we don't know!*

Obviously, David went through a meat grinder for these deeds. Obviously, God lifted His hand and made it clear that David got no free pass for the blatant premeditation of that series of ugliness (see 2 Sam. 12). But also, equally obvious, is that the Throne of David is the lineage that leads straight to King Jesus Christ.

On yet another side note, think about this: Whose sin was noteworthy enough for God to reject him as King of Israel: Saul's or David's? Saul's approval addiction or David's adultery and murder? Tell me, who would be preaching in your church next Sunday if this standard was applied today?

I want to be completely transparent with you. I've warred with approval addiction my whole life. On the other side of this spectrum, I love my wife and I will go to my grave being faithful to her out of that deep well of love. It staggers me that God has an altogether "other" view of what qualifies and disqualifies.

So why would I risk your attention to this treasured revelation of Radiance by inserting this matter? Why bother you with this potential point of contention? Because of something my dear spiritual father repeated: "Sometimes God will offend your mind to find your heart."

Whatever else this book may or may not be, *it is a work of the heart.* In order for it to come from my heart, and in order for it to reach the potential of hearts, I believe this line of probable offense must be defined.

I'm convinced that the entire prospect of high-profile fallen Christian leaders has been a significant impediment to our collective spiritual development for far too long! It seems to me that what we've seen in recent church history will continue to trip us up on multiple fronts *until* we choose new paths *forward.*

For my purposes here, I'm not talking about what associations, denominations, and networks have to do for whatever their criteria of discipline has to ferret out. I'm talking about the far more important issues of our transcendence of heart, the Radiance of His Kingdom through us, and the radical and sometimes scandalized nature of forgiveness and grace seizing the Body of Christ as a force of the immaterial world from which we were born!

In order for this to happen, we as individuals must take a flying leap over every offense and dive into the deep end of Jesus' radical behavior. Again, I'm not speaking here to an organization of bylaws and amendments, members and associates. I'm talking to you!

Where did you stop growing? What line of offense still has your toes edged to it? Whose failures are holding you in your own failure? Can you handle the reality that God may have drawn that very line to see if you would cross it in a pleading and bleeding pursuit of your unrealized potential? If your mind has been offended, *has God yet found your heart?*

Jesus drew the line of offense often. We would do well to learn His genius in it. For the rich young ruler, who certainly knew the Bible of his day and kept all the rules, Jesus dropped a Word of offense on him to work through before taking him any further (see Matt. 19:16-22). There was no "Bible" in leather-bound handiness to "flip" through, but I feel certain that the young man spent an inordinate amount of time flipping over and over in his mind just one thought, "But, I've kept the law! This isn't fair!"

In another incident, Jesus intentionally laid down a potential racial epithet in front of a Gentile woman who asked for her daughter's healing: *"It is not good to take the children's bread and throw it to the dogs"* (Matt. 15:26). Wow, that's scary by today's politically correct standards.

But this woman demonstrated an unwavering heart, which did not allow the offense to blockade her daughter's healing: *"Yes, Lord; but even the dogs feed on the crumbs which fall from their master's table"* (Matt. 15:27). Today's Christian culture is so loaded with self that 10,000 offenses are blockading 100,000 healings for sons and daughters. This woman's refusal to be offended became her act of faith: *"O woman, your faith is great; it shall be done for you as you wish"* (Matt. 15:28).

Self-pity is the antidote for your destiny.

Here's a Word for someone reading this at this very moment: what was once an offense to you can at this very moment become an act of faith if you will utterly refuse to live offended and treat that invective as incentive!

The day is upon us to refuse to allow offenses to blockade the raising up and healing of the next generation! For everyone who is reading this who longs to push on to seize your Kingdom potential, I say this is a vital line of potential offense—cross it and live!

Stay where you are and keep what you already have.

But if indeed you learn to read the Gospels honestly, you cannot miss the consistent pattern of Jesus drawing the line of potential offense over and over again. At every line there is yet another place for turning back and withering or clinging to Him and expanding your health and life.

I propose to you that you cannot un-father your father. Any attempt to do so is folly, at best, and sinful and life shortening, at worst (see Exod. 20:12; Eph. 6:1-2). Have you ever suffered through a reading of the genealogies in the Bible? If God wants the wide world to know the historical color and depth of the stories of our biblical lineage, what folly are we perpetuating when we currently jump from lineage to lineage, church to church, pretending to be what we are not?

Of course, we functionally move on when relationships may no longer be capable of sustaining process. But in the moving on, be sure that you are moving up, transcending the earthbound notions of fairness and disappointment. When *dis*-appointed, get *re*-appointed.

What would happen if a preponderance of the people of God stopped this flight from real and imagined embarrassments and stood in the midst of their spiritual families to be the genuinely spiritual who *restore* and are restored? (See Galatians 6:1-2.) What would happen if a determined remnant of us put an end to this repeating cycle, on both sides of these public failures, and chose a completely different path?

I believe we would start an avalanche of transgenerational, accelerated healing as we pass from one generation to the next our gifts and anointing so that God can multiply those same gifts and anointing, twofold, fourfold, and on and on!

I honestly don't know which is worse: (1) The sins and failures of high profile ministries or (2) The sins and failures of the Body of Christ in response to the aforementioned heartaches. I'm not talking about what law enforcement has to do, or what wrongs should justifiably be made right.

I'm talking about the collapse of the charitable, tangible grace that ought to be our most amazing trait! What would happen if we could find a more Christ-exalting, transcending Kingdom way in and through these matters?

I believe that if we did, the Kingdom of God would become more of the radiant dominance that would scatter and shatter the darkness, not only in our spiritual families, but more importantly, in a world of families living in dark shadows and aching for some elucidation from a Church that was always supposed to be the light of the world.

The core value I bring to you in this book is the good news of a Transcendent Supremacy that is in the presence and power of the Kingdom of God that is at your hand's reach. This heavenly reality is a tangible force to be reckoned with. This transcendence is so supreme that it affects the material world with transforming power, and it has vital energy and wisdom that will meet the needs of all humanity. As E. Stanley Jones says, "It is a total program for man's total life now."

That good news, however, demands something more of us than running from church to church, exposing sin, and the finger-pointing immaturity that has plagued us for far too long. Isaiah 58 clearly states that a true fast includes withholding the "pointing of the finger." Selling all for the Kingdom, for me, means the abandonment of my agenda and the surrender of my need to look good and protect my image.

I have a somewhat unique point of reference for all this. My mother went to an A.A. Allen tent crusade for prayer in 1952 in Tyler, Texas. Allen was a celebrated healing evangelist with a fairly high profile in those days.

My mother was determined to have a second child. She had some kind of medical procedure after which her doctor had told her that having a second baby was very risky at best and impossible at worst. Couple that with her knowledge that her own mother had died while giving birth, and you have the makings of why Mom made her way to an A.A. Allen healing crusade.

While there, she was delighted when she and my father received prayer and a prophecy from A.A. Allen. (Mom said that she floated down the aisle and realized later that Dad dutifully followed her.) Allen prophesied to her that she would successfully have a second child one year later. I am that second child, born in 1953.

A.A. Allen was a controversial figure, and some claimed, perhaps with some legitimacy and perhaps not, that he struggled with alcohol through many of his ministry years. I'm fairly certain that there are people who would gleefully suggest that he might have been drunk when he prayed for my mom. I can't prove anything on that regard this side of the time continuum, and frankly, for me it does not matter.

Here's what matters. Like the blind man in John 9 who said of Jesus, *"Whether He is a sinner, I do not know; one thing I do know, that, whereas I was blind, now I see."* Whatever else happened with A.A. Allen, I know this: I am a miracle, and God used that man miraculously in my parents' life when they were not faithful Christians.

This single reference point alone puts me at a distinctive vantage point. Like all of you, I have watched down through the years the rise and fall of dozens of ministries. I have wept, like some of you, when watching the painful parade of television evangelists and their embarrassments. I have, like some of you, grimaced recently, again and again, with more of the same. What are we to do?

First of all, learn well the lesson of Noah's three sons: Shem, Ham, and Japheth (see Gen. 9:20-27). After the flood Noah grew a vineyard, made wine, and got wasted. So bad was this drunk that he passed out naked. Ham finds his father in this embarrassing condition and he is immediately motivated into action…the wrong action.

You see, the problem here isn't that he told his other siblings. The problem here is that his *first* and most visceral point of action was to tell his other siblings. It was the honorable sons, Shem and Japheth, whose first reaction was to seize the moment to serve and not shame. So they walked into the room of their father's shame backward, so they could cover their father's drunken nakedness.

We don't know exactly all the nuances of the family dynamic, but clearly Ham is not feeling very charitable toward his father. Something in him is unresolved. His motivation seems more inclined to taking the old man down a notch than helping him in any way. Clearly something in Ham's soul is shrunken while the opposite is true of Shem and Japheth.

When Noah finds out what's been done he pronounces a curse that appears to me to be more of an acknowledgment of the outcome of character, or a lack thereof. In so many words Noah says that Ham's son, Canaan, will reflect the shrunken soul of his father.

Conversely, Noah blesses Shem and Japheth with an acknowledgment that their enlarged capacity for serving and kindness will enlarge their material world with the same. There's nothing so apt to reveal the internal realities of the children as a fallen or wounded parent.

When leaders fail, someone somewhere has to decide to do their own part to end the piranha-like feeding frenzy that clouds the water so much that it is impossible to distinguish between the eaten and the eater.

Secondly, give honor to whom and where honor is due (see Rom. 13:7). *Honor the king* (1 Pet. 2:17) was written in a day when kings could be pagan monsters. How can this be? Because, I believe that honor given is holy humility received, regardless of the worthiness in the object of your honoring behavior. The honor I train my heart to live in is much more about healing for me than it is about any other factor involved in the relationship in which I find myself. Basic Christian discipleship has always been about growing dimensions of obedience, humility, and servanthood. Few matters in life challenge these realities more than our relationships with and responses to authority.

What about our reaction to corrupt or damaged authority? Pilate and Herod make today's politicians look like Johnny Appleseed by comparison, yet Jesus kept His own dignity intact in their presence. His razor-sharp discernment and knowledge of their personal lives could have served up an exposé more telling than any ambush news reporter of our day could begin to imagine. But rather than raising His voice in shame, He quieted His soul in serenity. His coming Radiant Resurrection was all the response He would need.

The greatest danger for our own hearts in the face of these kinds of challenges is that we unwittingly devalue our own sensibilities and this in the name of Christ!

Will we continue this insanity of self-defense or transcend the obvious and seize the sublime?

As I am writing these words, there is a loud cultural debate about profanity in music. What amazes me is that some of the people arguing for toning down the language of musicians are some of the same people speaking profane and harsh words about politicians and many in authority with whom they disagree. Disagree all you want to, but guard your heart from the calcifying effects of dishonor. It is fascinating to me how we can clearly see end results without noticing our own participation in the process.

C.S. Lewis said:

> You can hardly open a periodical without coming across the statement that what our civilization needs is more 'drive,' or dynamism, or self-sacrifice, or 'creativity.' In a sort of ghastly simplicity we remove the organ and demand the function. We make men without chests and expect of them virtue and enterprise. We laugh at honor and are shocked to find traitors in our midst. We castrate (the beast) and bid the geldings be fruitful.[1]

We live in an honor-deprived culture. From late show comedians who make a living spoofing presidents, politicians, and preachers to music and games celebrating violence, our culture is marinating in dishonor. But Second Peter 2:9-16 is a striking indictment that warns us against being dishonoring even against the most dishonorable. Why? Because we marginalize the potential beauties of our own soul by coarse behavior toward any in authority, and we minimize the potential of healthy honor coming back to us should we live in a manner that might merit true honor.

I have come to believe that this is a hidden curse that invites a "bushel" to hide the light of our potentially world-changing enlightened radiance. Jesus gave us the most incredible prophetic compliment when He called us *"the light of the world"* (see Matt. 5). The fact is that as we read the beautiful attitudes of the beatitudes throughout the Sermon on the Mount, we cannot help but be struck by the enlargement of spirit and soul that Jesus is offering humankind if we will turn cheeks, walk second miles, make peace, and be blessed in the face of insults! The result is that we will be ***radiant*** *lights like a city on a hill, seen for miles!*

Yet, on we live in an honor-deprived culture, and out of this deprivation an abnormality has appeared in too many Christian circles. This oddity is expressed in a greater concern on our part for the potential abuses, however great or slight, that someone in authority might get away with; all the while we remain largely ignorant of our own self-abuse that shrinks our hearts into cynical vessels of stony harshness and crude arrogance.

Why would I refer to this as an oddity? Because one of the baseline principles of Christ's teaching is that the speck in your brother's eye may indeed be the two-by-four stuck in your own eye. How do we read these Kingdom truths and teach these transcendent realities all the while violating them as we proclaim them?

Perhaps, worst of all, we shrink the possibilities of genuine apostles, prophets, evangelists, pastors, and teachers from the discipling task of pressing us toward the measure of the full stature of Jesus Christ (see Eph. 4:11-13). When God says that His gifts and callings are irrevocable (see Rom. 11:29), what harm have we done to ourselves when we revoke the influence of a spiritual father or mother with unconditional and irrevocable severity?

Dishonor for authority we see is ultimately dishonor for authority we cannot see. Exodus 22:28 states, *"You shall not curse God, nor a ruler of your people,"* and is a timeless truth because God knows the propensity of the human condition that fails to draw healthy lines for our own good between earthly and heavenly authority.

In response to the inevitable accusation that my words here could be taken as license for leadership to sin, I have one thing to say: People looking for a license to sin would find a license to sin in a nursery rhyme. Regardless, make no mistake about it, I believe that we have all (leaders and followers alike) wasted too much of God's good time selling our souls for moments of stupidity given to those sins and, equally, to the moments of denouncing the sinners! (Later in this book pay particular attention to the chapter entitled "Mud Pie Indigestion.")

We all need to grow up beyond our arrested development and, for Heaven's sake, live free and forward.

There is nothing in these words that should be construed as condoning the sins of leadership. It's time to double only the good of what a previous generation has done, and let those who are dead bury the dead works of a previous generation so that the Kingdom of God can finally come on earth, as it is in Heaven!

I routinely tell my flock, "Watch me! Like the apostle Paul, I offer myself as a model (see 2 Thess. 3:9). If I fall, watch me get up! But if I stand, imitate my walk and vibrate Kingdom reality everywhere the soles of your feet tread."

So what would I do if someone in my pastoral care crosses a line and pours too much honor at my feet? I would do what the brother did in Revelation 19:10 when he stopped the great apostle John from worshiping him by saying, *"Do not do that...worship God."* Not very complicated: honor for humans and worship for God. But isn't it interesting that John is corrected for giving *too much* honor. I'll take that correction any day over being a shrunken critical soul who has hardly begun to honor, much less give too much.

I believe it was Dietrich Bonhoeffer who said, "Many Christians are unthinkably horrified when a real sinner is suddenly discovered among the righteous. So we remain alone with our sin, living in lies and hypocrisy...."

I so long to give my church a model to live transparently and to know that the glory of the Kingdom's presence is thick enough to cover all our nakedness while we heal from any of our failures.

In this book I am crying out for the Church, particularly in America, to take a flying leap over the multiple potential offenses, past, present, and surely to come, and reach the potential of our radiance: a Transcendent Supremacy of

Kingdom influence that dominates a room or a region for Christ. While we hear much about the dangers of "burn-out," I am more concerned that we have suffered and even tolerated a spiritual "brown-out" as normal Christian life. I say that whatever darkness may come is a dare for us to "Arise and only shine" (see Isa. 60:1)!

Regardless of what has been shouted from the roof-tops, Bishop Earl Paulk remains regarded by me as a spiritual father. He is deserving of my honor to him for braving the heat of the day, and birthing in me, and in tens of thousands, the message of the Kingdom of God that impassions me to this very moment. The words he whispered in my ear the day he and his presbytery ordained me still resonate in my heart: "I accept the responsibility of watching over your soul." It is my honor to repeat the fathering power of those words in the hearts of my sons and daughters who now trust me with their ordination.

May God grant me grace to run hard after Him all the days of my life, and to relay a torch of bonfire quality and quantity to the next generation, daring them to take that torch of Radiance and *double it!*

ENDNOTE

1. C.S. Lewis, *The Abolition of Man: Reflections on education with special reference to the teaching of English in the upper forms of schools.* http://www.columbia.edu/cu/augustine/arch/lewis/abolition1.htm.

Chapter 3

A Transcendental Meditation (Transcendence and Presence)

We aren't humans on a spiritual path.
We are spirits on a human path.
—Unknown

We all know people who make us feel better about ourselves just being around them. I'm with one of those people right now on a flight to Mexico for a mission trip. This guy makes you want to laugh because his free and easy laughter creates that kind of environment. For arduous trips like the one we are on, he is our secret weapon of the joy of the Lord which infuses us with strength. The truth be told, I almost feel guilty going on a mission trip with him because we have such a good time when we are supposed to be "sacrificing."

OK, there—now I'm over the guilt.

We also know people who have the opposite effect. Their presence is laced with tension, strife, and generalized negativity. Their company, even without a word spoken, is like a black hole whose gravitational pull will bend every topic discussed. You're glad when the meeting you are in with them is over, and even when it's over, there is a residual effect. Everyone is tired and drained and checking their calendar so they can start thinking of excuses early on to miss the next meeting.

The premise of this book is rooted in that understanding of who we are, but the long-range, far-reaching implications are much more involved. I believe that one of Christianity's least-known and least-explored powers (but perhaps one of its most revolutionary concepts) is that of Transcendence and Presence. If people consistently and for the most part unintentionally create such energy and atmosphere around them, it should be no stretch to know and understand God and His Kingdom in the same way.

God is the source of everything created, which means every living thing has, is, and will always have the taproot of life from Him. He is unlimited in every conceivable notion of power, creativity, dynamic, force, and pure raw energy. So I believe that it is NO stretch of the imagination to think of Him as having a pure environmental influence, which creates a tangible and experientially proven presence.

If the disaster in Chernobyl could leave a region ruined by nuclear radiation, doesn't it stand to a healthy reasoning that, in a completely opposite manner, God would far and away influence anyone and anything He touches or even comes near with life and health? Even pressing the nuclear plant accident analogy further, the origination point of that nuclear power is God Himself.

I'll say it again: He is Radiance (see Heb. 1:1-3; Hab. 3:4). What surrounds Him is The Radiance. Come into that vortex and you change. (See Malachi 4:2. The healing "wings" referred to in this passage are like the rays of light shooting off the sun.) Carry that Radiance with you, and your surroundings are profoundly impacted. Multiply that Radiance through faith, prayer, and most importantly, intimate covenant relationship, and a neighborhood, a region, a state, and a nation are ultimately changed. God's goal, which should be ours, is that the whole earth is changed under the Radiance of this Transcendent Supremacy.

REBUKED BY PROMISE

When the Israelites retreated from the idea of going into the Promised Land with the excuse that they felt like grasshoppers in their own eyes, God rebuked them with a promise (see Num. 14:21). Through Moses, He prophesied a day when the whole earth would be filled with the glory of God as the waters cover the sea. Context here is everything. It starts with the notion of conquering a small patch of land and ends with a promise for the whole earth.

There was no thought in the mind of God that the Promised Land would just suddenly "convert" in one giant catastrophic moment. And there is no thought in the mind of God today that His glory will cover the earth only after some series of "end-times" catastrophes. That glory, that Radiance, that Transcendent Supremacy of the Kingdom of God comes only from our active participation to spread it.

We are the potential bearers of the glory of God throughout the whole earth. This essence of the Kingdom's reality is what can truly set us apart from mere religious thinkers. Bearing this magnificence with humble intentionality dominates a room or a region with all the benefits of the Kingdom's beauty and deliverance. Christ in us is the hope of that glory (see Col. 1:27).

I am more and more convinced that a significant revelation must come to the people of God in order for that Glory and Radiance to become a reality. Jesus said in Matthew 5:14-16:

> You are the light of the world. A city set on a hill cannot be hidden; nor does anyone light a lamp and put it under a basket, but on the lampstand, and it gives light to all who are in the house. Let your light shine before men in such a way that they may see your good works, and glorify your Father who is in heaven.

Our light is the conduit that links an unbelieving world with Heaven. Our light is the potential incentive for an unbelieving world to shout, "Glory to God!" I believe it was Charles Simpson who said, "It's one thing for the Church to say, 'glory to God,' but I'm looking forward to the day when the world around us sees God's work in and through us and *they* say, 'glory to God!'"

When we bring the atmosphere of the Holy Spirit, we bring the prevailing influence of the Kingdom of God. Romans 14:17 says that the Kingdom of God is in the Holy Spirit's character and environment of righteousness, peace, and joy. These three qualities are prevailing, positive-pressure systems that improve any sphere they are allowed to enlighten. Let your light shine.

In Exodus 33:16 Moses literally bargained with God for a clear transcendent reality of His presence with Israel, saying, *"For how then can it be known that I have found favor in Your sight, I and Your people? Is it not by Your going with us, so that we, I and Your people, may be distinguished from all the other people who are upon the face of the earth?"* He is saying, "God, be the Transcendent Supremacy of our very existence! When the nations of the earth see us, let them see You radiantly, luminously shining above all of our other realities."

From the entire context of that experience, we are unflinchingly told in Second Corinthians 3 that a greater Transcendent Supremacy is potentially upon us today and that this supreme reality has the efficacy to transform everything in its wake! In fact, in this chapter Paul rhetorically asked in verse 8, *"How will the ministry of the Spirit fail to be even more with glory?"*

RADIANCE IS OUR DESTINY!

Zechariah 8:23 says, *"Thus says the Lord of hosts, 'In those days ten men from all the nations will grasp the garment of a Jew, saying, "Let us go with you, for we have heard that God is with you."'"* Other similar promises flirt with us to imagine people coming from faraway places who bow down before us without even knowing our names because *"God is with you."* (See Isaiah 45:14; 60:14.)

Indeed, Micah 4 brazenly declares that the Transcendent Reign of God's Kingdom upon lame, afflicted outcasts will induce the nations of the world to spend their war treasure chests on agricultural production! Now that's Transcendent Supremacy!

For another dispensation you say? I say, the devil does not care what you believe about a fantasy future. He will give you a wide berth of delightful detachment to sing about that glorious day, someday, waaaaaay out there as long as he can keep the aforementioned outcasts in his bondage and the nations of the world loading their guns with hatred today.

Furthermore, I say that the day everything changes is the day that a hungry, passionate band of hardcore Kingdom believers wraps their faith around promises like Micah 4, Jeremiah 33:9, Ephesians 1:9,10; 3:1-21, Revelation 5, and others too many to list at this point. Our influence, light, inspiration, stimulus, and bearing on the atmosphere of our world are potentially without boundaries.

"Nation will arise against nation" (Matt. 24:7) is not some script that God has written for the creation of an end-time's machinery irrevocably locked into a catastrophic climax! These "signs" are not for the purpose of unplugging us from responsibility for the day in which we live. Indeed, Jesus referred to these signs as a necessity for the birth of something that would be the ultimate solution! *"But all these things are merely the beginning of birth pangs.... But the one who endures to the end, he will be saved. This gospel of the kingdom shall be preached in the whole world as a testimony to all the nations, and then the end will come"* (Matt. 24:8;13-14).

While we are on the subject of signs, particularly the ones I just mentioned, I am personally convinced that Jesus was simply laying out for us the grid of what has been true throughout world history. Every generation since He spoke these words has seen exactly what He said we would see!

Look again at this chapter in Matthew that's been abused too often. If there is any sign of anything defined here, it is the sign of the way we were and are. In the middle of all our uproar, however, He says that someone will endure and the Gospel of the Kingdom will be communicated and demonstrated.

Not just the gospel of "if you were to die tonight, will you go to Heaven or hell." But the Kingdom Gospel that says, "If by some chance *you live* for many more decades to come, will you live a hellish existence, making no difference in this world of hell's domination? *If you live,* will you die to self, take up a purpose far greater than self, sell all your agendas for the sake of the Kingdom, and *live a witness of Heaven's* dominion on you, in you, and through you into *all* the world? We call on you this day to bow your knee to Jesus Christ and believe and cry out from the deepest ache of your heart, 'Jesus Christ is Lord!' God raised Him from the dead so that you could live and become a raging river of resurrection Life to the world around you!" (See Romans 10:9-10.)

Evangelical Christianity has searched and researched for the best outreach tools to "win the lost at any cost." Sometimes these schemes work best, albeit short-term, as church attendance ploys. At their worst, and most often, they are just plain manipulative. Wouldn't the more excellent way be if everywhere we walked and lived, due to the overwhelmingly compelling beauty of God's environmental influence upon us, people are drawn to us like metal filings to a magnet?

In Mark 1:14-28 we read an amazing account of this irresistible, compelling beauty at work through Jesus. First, He throws into the air the blast of the Spirit's intention: *"The time is fulfilled, and the Kingdom of God is at hand; repent and believe in the Gospel."* Something cracks wide open throughout the land, He walks up to His first choices for disciples, and says, *"Follow Me...,"* and they are thunderstruck so profoundly that they throw down their means of financial support (fishing nets) and immediately abandon themselves to this teacher they had just met moments before!

Folks, that's the Transcendent Supremacy of the authority in Christ that founded His movement and should *still* be founding His Church if we *too* will believe the Gospel (Good News) of the immediacy of this domain that has come to possess every tribe and nation! Later in this reference, the crowds observing Jesus said, "What is this? A new teaching with authority!" This says to me that the very air He spoke into was crackling with the energy of the Kingdom of the heavens.

I propose to you that we have traded our treasures for trinkets when we allow these and a multitude of other Scriptures to be hijacked away for a millennial dispensation far removed from our responsibility for faith. It is my heartfelt belief and passion that our greatest evangelistic reality is that of the Kingdom of God and its Transcendence and Presence.

In Mark 2:1-4 we are told that when word got out that Jesus was in a particular home, a crowd put that home under siege and tore a hole in the roof to get a sick man near Jesus. In Luke 15:1 we are told that complete strangers to the religious order of the day were flocking to get as close to Jesus as they could, just to hear the Transcendent Supremacy in His voice. Jesus said in Luke 16:16 that the Word of His Kingdom was so compelling and energized that, *"everyone* [yes, He said *EVERYONE*] *is forcing his way into it* [the Kingdom]."

And speaking of Dr. Luke...

Chapter 4

A Physician's Vision for Solving a Health Care Crisis

D r. Luke must have been freaking out as he watched thousands of tormented, disturbed, and just generally sick people crowding around Jesus. Think about it. Two thousand years ago, if you were sick on *any* level, *you were sick!* A bad cut could kill you. An impacted tooth could kill you. There was no such thing as antibiotics, aspirin, Band-Aids, stitches, vaccinations, tetanus shots, and the list just keeps going on and on. That doesn't even begin to mention antidepressants or any other kind of help for the psychologically needy person.

One of the words used in Luke's Gospel to describe some of the throngs crowding around Jesus was the Greek word *nosos* (in Luke 6:18), which had a notion of being morally messed up. Another word used was *asthenia* (in Luke 4:40), which could include being painfully backward and mostly emotionally feeble. Disturbed and scary is how we might put it.

Nice group of folks, huh? And we are talking herds, packs, pulsing, pushing, grabbing masses. Oh, and one other thing: personal hygiene. Deodorant, toothpaste, daily baths? Forget about it.

But beyond that collective, crusty mass of humanity, Dr. Luke records his astonishment at what was happening to these people: *"And all the people* [the multitude] *were trying to touch him, for power was coming from Him and healing them all"* (Luke 6:19); *"...laying His hands on each one of them, He was healing them"* (Luke 4:40); *"large crowds were gathering to hear Him and to be healed of their sicknesses"* (Luke 5:15); and *"the power of the Lord was present for Him to perform healing"* (Luke 5:17).

Dr. Luke seems to be painting a word picture of a Transcending Presence It was as though radiance or a transcendent power was pushing and pulsing through crowds like a giant beam of creativity making broken lives completely well! Jesus was giving off this "force field" of health, well-being, and wholeness that was more contagious than the sicknesses which were being eradicated.

Indeed, I imagine that if the good doctor had been physically present in this moment, he would have held his breath when Jesus stood over Peter's mother-in-law who was *"suffering from a high fever"* (Luke 4:38). I suspect that Luke would have been taking an internal inventory of what medication he might have had on hand in the event that everyone in this party would catch whatever caused this fever. In the middle of his mental listing, however, he would have heard Jesus rebuke the fever, and his medical reasoning would have had to stand down long enough for him to record in simplicity, with regard to the fever, "…*and it left her*" (Luke 4:39). The fever was displaced by a greater contagion: the Kingdom of God in the presence of Jesus.

"And it left her? What's that you said, doctor? Could you please simplify your medical jargon a bit? If I didn't know any better, I could have sworn that you just said that the fever instantaneously went away."

In one location, so many people were profoundly impacted by this aura that they were quite naturally begging Jesus to stay. His response summarizes my theme here: "*I must preach the kingdom of God to the other cities also, for I was sent for this purpose*" (Luke 4:43). Dr. Luke's cataloging of these mind-boggling events is the chronicle of what the Kingdom of God does in people and how it influences a region.

What does this mean to me? It means I want to become a bearer of that Radiance! And not only that, but I want to start a revolution of that kind of Transcendent Supremacy. If the Chernobyl disaster can leave a sickening radiation field for 10,000 years, then how much more can the resurrection of Christ produce a domination of health that can send holy shock waves through a region?

Charles Spurgeon once said:

> It would be easy to show that at our present rate of progress the kingdoms of this world never could become the Kingdom of our Lord and of His Christ. Indeed, many in the Church are giving up on the idea of it except on the occasion of the advent of Christ, which, as it chimes in with our own idleness, is likely to be a popular doctrine. I myself believe that King Jesus will reign, and the idols be utterly abolished; but I expect the same power which turned the world upside down once will still continue to do it. The Holy Ghost would never suffer the imputation to rest upon His holy name that He was not able to convert the world.[1]

If the kingdoms of this world are to "become the Kingdom of our Lord and of His Christ" (see Rev. 11:15), then somebody needs to start something that is seriously buckling some knees. I can't speak for anyone else, but I can say for myself, I desperately want this kind of Kingdom reality in and around me. Church status quo in this regard has now become part of the sickness of our society, and it must stop now.

Enough! I cry out, *"Thy kingdom come, Thy will be done on earth as it is in heaven."* I am glad you've joined me at least this far, but hang on tight…I've just begun to share my own journey in this Radiance of the Kingdom. More lines of offense may fall at your feet. Dogmas of a tired past will be targeted.

Many years ago I was an assistant pastor in a church struggling to survive itself. That's right, survive *itself*.

On one hand they had enjoyed several months of incredible growth due to their very real love for God and a hunger for His presence. When I first arrived, new converts were being baptized in water every week. As a result the atmosphere was wonderfully chaotic with baby Christians everywhere.

On the other hand the leadership was amazingly dysfunctional. When we ran out of things to argue about, we simply invented new and improved ways to argue. At one meeting two of the most opinionated men in the room jumped to their feet and charged at each other like two rams in a nature film. I was so stunned by what I was watching that I sat transfixed as if waiting for a bell to ring. Fortunately for all of us, by the time they were nose to nose they realized the ugliness of what they were about to do.

Before long, the senior pastor left, and I was suddenly in charge at the ripe old age of 23. Even though I didn't know what to call it, I knew enough about transcendence then to know that whatever else we were going to do, we were going to ramp up our pursuit for the presence of God.

God was faithful, even as we were not. Leadership meetings got worse, but worship got better. Go figure.

After too many weeks of this, I was completely exhausted. One day I got up from my desk and dragged myself into the sanctuary and just lay face down on the stage.

"God!" I cried into the carpet, "You've got to give me a reason to keep doing this!"

Silence.

After waiting for a reason and getting none, I got up, cleaned the carpet, and wiped my nose...or was it the other way around? Nevertheless...

On my way out of the building I stopped at the place we kept incoming mail and noticed a recent letter with my name on it. The contents went something like this:

Dear Pastor Randy,

You don't know me, but I was in your church a month ago. I own a business and frequently have to travel by car past your location. Many years ago I was in a terrible auto accident that almost paralyzed me. To this day I have horrible pain in my back. I take multiple drugs for this condition and, routinely, I have to get pain shots just to get through a day. While I am not a strong believer, I do have a basic respect for God's existence. On the Sunday I was driving past your church, my back pain was overwhelming. I considered driving to the nearest emergency room for a shot when I saw your church and a voice said, "Stop here and I'll heal you." I was desperate and willing to try anything. Your evening service had already begun; I slipped in unnoticed and sat in the back row. I have never been to a church like yours before. The instant I walked in I felt a Presence that I have never known. When I sat down I immediately knew that my back was getting better. By the time your service was finished I was completely well! Frankly, I was somewhat embarrassed by my emotions so I slipped out and finished my journey. It is now over a month later and I have not needed any shots for pain and I have almost completely eliminated using my prescriptions.

Whatever it is you do there, keep it up! Thank you.

That letter became my Word from God. It also taught me a valuable lesson about "doing church." Whatever else we do, we absolutely must become a people and a place on earth where God's presence is more real than our buildings. Bill Johnson says, "God will give us the level of His presence that we will jealously guard."

I read that letter at our next leadership meeting. I told them that if they couldn't give up Tuesday Night Fight Night that they should resign and make room for somebody who would respect the presence of God in our church. To my shock and surprise, one by one each man resigned over the next few weeks and the presence of God in that place was indeed respected.

(It should be noted here that I have since learned that ultimatums are not the best form of leadership development, particularly with guys present who might otherwise be prone to throwing fists. I was 23 and exhausted. God must have served popcorn that night in the heavenly viewing room as members of the cloud of witnesses gathered for the potential entertainment.)

There's a contrast to be observed here. Jesus lived out the full momentum of the Transcendent Supremacy of His Father's Kingdom, and the vibrations set up shock waves of health and wholeness. In my story of the First Church of the Blessed Chaos we were stumbling and fumbling our way into the Kingdom Come. Jesus did it intentionally and we did it incidentally. The time has come for us all to do it with a complete passionate intentionality.

In his poem *After the Storm,* Boris Pasternak (author of the epic novel, *Doctor Zhivago*) wrote in 1958 these words which capture my intention:

> It is not revolutions and
> upheavals That clear the road to new
> and better days, But revelations,
> lavishness and torments Of someone's
> soul, inspired and ablaze.[2]

An old African American preacher said it more simply, "These things are better 'caught' than taught." So: come along with me as I continue to relate my journey.

Let's catch what Jesus had.

ENDNOTES

1. Charles Spurgeon, quoted in David Chilton, *Paradise Restored* (Reconstruction Press, 1985), 129.

2. Boris Pasternak, "After the Storm" (1958), from *Fifty Poems,* trans. by Lydia Pasternak Slater (1963).

Chapter 5

How Dare We Be Powerless?

As of the writing of this chapter I am a week out from the honor of speaking at another youth camp. I'm spent, but everything in me is shaking with desire. My mind, will, and emotions are stormy. The Holy Spirit is flying in and around my vision. I can't shake the lump in my throat, and frankly, I don't want to. Work with me for a few moments and maybe I can make some sense of it with the following words.

Youth camps typically bring students out of some sampling of our society's misery. This camp was no different. But what was different for me, at any rate, is that I've been focused on the call and ministry of Moses and how he miraculously led Israel out of Egypt. God has had me dipped in the various nuances of what happened: a shepherd's staff becomes "the rod of God" and eats serpents, splits seas, and generally shakes a world superpower into surrender. (One note here would be helpful: I'm not saying that I

73

preached out of this story for this particular camp. I'm saying I have been nourishing my heart, soul, and mind with these truths. The greatest enemy to my Christian life can become my Christian ministry when, among other things, I default to studying to "preach." Of quality education it has been said, "Don't fill pails; light fires." The same holds true here.)

After our week of camp was done and I sat listening to these teenagers share their stories, my heart cracked wide open and my eyes haven't stopped pouring a river of prayer ever since. One young lady related how she was determined to keep what God had done in her life that week. She talked about my challenge to the campers to be the bearers of a Transcendent Supremacy that would not only push back the darkness, but crush it! Then she went on to say that last year she had a similar determination, but an adult met her at her home door and physically beat her for being so "happy." The likelihood that I would contribute to any remote possibility of sending her home without the backing of a universal church full of world-overcoming power is repugnant to me.

How dare we, the Church of the Risen Lord, be powerless? How can we accept our impotency in the face of the raging devourer who is eating children and families alive? What excuses will we bear in our trembling hands before our Father when He asks an account of our stewardship of His Kingdom on earth? He declared that His Kingdom will ultimately become the Kingdom of this earth, that *every* knee will ultimately bow and *every* tongue will ultimately confess and that there is a surpassing greatness of His power aimed at us who believe, which is the same power that raised Jesus from the dead. Yet, we are all too often powerless in Pharaoh's presence as he slumps in his throne and giggles under his breath at our demands to release God's people.

Please don't read in my words any shame or blame at you who give me the time to read this word. I join you in an inventory, which requires me to ask real questions in order to find real answers. Last week, while I saw some physical and spiritual healings that made me dance with joy, I also heard stories of teenagers who will go home to the potential of hell greeting them at the door. I gave as much instruction as I know to go home with power and confidence, but I also know that the rest of us, on the outside of those stories, must be equally, if not more, empowered in order to become part of a tipping point in history!

Which one of us will be that tipping point? What moment of deep calling out to deep in God will light a burning bush? Who will open his or her spiritual eyes to see God, high and lifted up, at precisely the right tick of the clock that will cause the pillars of the Throne to shake at the cry for justice on earth from the God whose Holy character will not long wait to heal the great leprosy of the children of His making?

He baits us up into His presence that He might ask, "Whom shall I send and who will go for Me? Have you dared to live long enough *now* with tokens of My power? Are you ready now for a burning coal of Heaven to permanently blister every word you speak?" (See Isaiah 6.)

I dared my church yesterday with these words: "The culture of unbelief we live in demands a faith and a believing from us that is uncommon so that we might put on display a God we can never intellectualize or debate a watching world into believing." Nature itself abhors a vacuum. If you or I were somehow able to suck all the air out of a little jar and put a lid on it, every square inch of the atmosphere surrounding the earth would go to work to crush that jar and invade it with oxygen.

The lack of spiritual air in our day and time is an implosion waiting to happen!

In the fullness of time, God sent His Son (see Gal. 4:4). Now, in another fullness of time, we are here in this hour.

How dare we be powerless? Indeed. Right at this moment, I dare you to be powerful. I dare you to drop this book to the floor and then join the book on the floor crying out for more of the Holy Spirit than you've ever known before. Rise from the floor if and when you must, but do not part from that quest.

Chapter 6

ALWAYS AT YOUR BEST?

Only the mediocre are always at their best.
—Unknown Texas Preacher

B
ack in the middle 1980s, the Dean family lived in Austin, Texas, one of the coolest towns on earth. Art and entertainment venues, natural eye-popping sights, and a variety of people and cultural types live in one of the best-kept city secrets in America. I'm proud to say I lived there even for a short time. One of the best and free entertainment spots was the State of Texas Capitol.

I went there at least once a week to pray and people-watch. When the legislature was in session, the variety show was better than anything on television. One time, sitting in the balcony and watching the dog-and-pony show on the main floor, I was laughing hard and trying not to be a disruption.

Suddenly from behind me someone tapped me on the shoulder, and I thought I was going to be kicked out. Instead, I turned around and there was Ann Richards (then State Treasurer, soon to be Governor and nationally a Democratic Party power player) laughing with me. Through her own laughter and with a sophisticated southern accent, she said, "Pretty good show, isn't it?"

Not long after that incident I was in that same spot when a local Baptist preacher was asked to open the session with prayer. His words were short and riveting. He took the podium, simply said, "Let us pray," and proceeded to hit a grand slam with one of the shortest prayers I've ever heard: "Lord, remind us today that only the mediocre are always at their best. Amen." The legislative floor was stunned into unusual silence. I wanted to laugh and all at once shout, "Amen" at the top of my lungs!

Allow me to take a leap of truth from that statement and offer my own: *I would rather fail at attempting the miraculous than succeed at mediocrity.* I often tell my church to sing loudly and "If you make a mistake, please make a loud one!" That's a pretty good rule for life too.

Another youth camp I recently ministered to had as its theme, "Finding Our Voice." They were challenged to find their own voice by the power of the Holy Spirit, and to attempt to have the transcendent supernatural power of God resonate through their lifestyle. It's good fun to take the risk with young people and dare them out of living their faith in a sterile, vanilla package. If we all know that God is "big," why do we all live so small? Being arrogant is silly and repugnant, but so is playing small when we serve such an expansive and extraordinary God.

One story that came out of this camp was about a group of teenage boys who were praying into the wee hours of the morning after an evening service. I had spoken that night about Jesus' own Transcendence and the unlimited Life that He lived. In the middle of their prayer time, the suggestion came up that if Jesus could walk through walls, we should too. So, one boy got up, prayed, and walked full force into a door. The door did not yield. He picked himself up, declared it must be his lack of faith, and took off for the door again. The door won again, but this little band of brothers was not discouraged. Though their guinea pig brother had enough bruises for the moment, they declared that someday they were going to win this challenge!

Oh, I can already hear the murmur of the religiously mediocre: "Someone should instruct these children to temper their expectations." Why? So that we can kidnap the next generation to remain at the level of our own status quo, and thereby validate our impotence as normal? An old rabbinical proverb says, "Don't limit a child to your own learning for he was born in another time."

Just as our children and grandchildren are entering a global economy dominated by technology only dreamed of in years previous, so the current day version of Pharaoh's magicians continue to own the attention of too many youthful royal courts. ENOUGH!

I say to the boys I mentioned here and to an entire generation, "Keep experimenting with your faith, boys and girls...wear a helmet if you'd like, but don't quit! One day, you'll get something right and Pharaoh's serpents will be consumed by a shepherd's staff again" (see Exod. 7).

My point here is that for too long Christianity has allowed for a mediocrity at almost every level of its expression. We screwed up the motto, "Failure is not an option," by reversing it into a call to be safe and never daring. Essential components of Christianity have been marginalized, diluted, tamed, domesticated, and even brazenly eliminated down through the years for the purposes of mainstreaming the message. While I certainly believe that the truths of Christ are for the everyday person, I also believe that our efforts to get it there have stopped far short of that noble goal.

In fact, many of these means have become the goal. The bridges that cross the obstacles have become the destination. We've gathered masses onto the bridges when the road is stretched out in front of us as far as the eye can see!

A simple way of expressing this is in a statement I heard many years ago, "We are either doing the works of Jesus or we are spending most of our time explaining why we aren't and why we can't."

I would rather fail at attempting the miraculous than to succeed at mediocrity. Good has always been the greatest enemy of the best, and our best was never intended to be leveled-off at mediocrity.

We are the bearers of an insuperable sovereignty. We are potentially radiant with a Holy Spirit World of invulnerable and pervasive force. I believe that one of our most hidden dreads is that we won't rise to the promise of the presence of the Kingdom of God in our world. This would explain to me why Jesus would say, *"Do not be afraid, little flock, for your Father has chosen gladly to give you the kingdom"* (Luke 12:32).

Imagine if I were to tell my friends that I plan on achieving a perfect score in gymnastics at the next Olympics. A good friend might point out to me that I am not capable of doing a chin-up, much less a perfect routine on the high bar. Another friend might helpfully suggest that I enter a local gymnastics competition first.

With my hands on my hips I could throw my head back in derisive laughter and say, "How foolish! My perfect score will come on that glorious day when every eye will see and every tongue confess that the great Ran-DEE is god of the high bar! HA-HA! Be gone from me, you fools."

The only fool in this story would of course be me. But isn't this how we have massaged the Scriptures into a grand and glorious finish at the return of Jesus with no Glorious Church in the meantime?

Ladies and gentlemen, the King is already seated in His exalted Throne! Let every other poser of power be bound, and let every benefit of His dominance be loosed! (See Matthew 18:18.) If the end of all things is His Kingdom's complete success (see Rev. 11:15), then the present must at the very least become an adequate witness and a tangible demonstration of just how excellent and remarkable that end will be.

In fact, there can be no "end" until throughout all the world and in all of its systems the Gospel of the *Kingdom* is heralded, not just with words, but in a witnessed demonstration! (See Matthew 24:14.)

Chin-ups, anyone?

Chapter 7

EXPECTATIONS AND DISAPPOINTMENTS

We tend to water down our expectations
to the level of our disappointments.
—Randy Dean

If we are not diligent, we tend to water down our expectations to the level of our disappointments. Pastor Kris Vallotton of Bethel Church in Redding, California, says it this way: "When your memories are greater than your dreams, you've already begun to die." To be a "believer" is just that, folks, to be a *believer!* We ought to be saying to a watching world, "Hey! Look over here…We believe stuff!"

It is potentially a wild privilege to be a believer in a culture of unbelief. Nature abhors a vacuum. As I wrote earlier, if you were able to suck all the air out of a small jar and successfully put a lid on it, all of the air circling the planet from the surface of that jar to the limits of the stratosphere would all at once wage war to crush that little jar.

The vacuum that unbelief creates is an amazing opportunity for people of faith to step forward with the clarity of a contrast. In Matthew 24:14, Jesus makes it clear that before any kind of an "end" to anything, God seeks someone who will clearly preach the Kingdom of God and then live a witness as a demonstration.

In another place, Luke 10:9, Jesus told His disciples to heal the sick and tell them that the Kingdom came near enough to do the healing. This tells me that the Kingdom of God holds explosive spiritual treasures waiting for the hungry, curious, insatiably and voraciously eager seeker who comes with irresistible desire.

Furthermore, the spread of this Kingdom aura is as elementary as speaking and going places. Do you have a voice? Do you go places? If the answer is yes, then everywhere you go, speak, *"Peace to this house* [business, school, store, airport, etc.]*…and heal those in it who are sick, and say to them, 'The Kingdom of God has come near to you'"* (Luke 10:5,9).

How many times have I heard people commiserate that they don't know what to say to people about their faith. Here's a thought—say, "Peace." Why not with a simple heart plug the Transcendent Supremacy of the Kingdom of God into that word and see what God will do. *Radiate peace!*

I've been blessed to be elected to my sixth term of service on a local public school board. I've learned much more than I've taught in that role and I'll forever be grateful for the privilege of serving my local community. But one thing is a sure thing when you serve in any public setting… you *will* tick somebody off somewhere at sometime for something. In fact, I tell people that by being a pastor I can only offend people in just a few counties but by being on a board of education I can spread my influence and offend people from an entire region!

Anyway, I had one person recently (at least one) who was especially unhappy with me for a tough decision our board had to make. He wrote me, called me, came to my office, came to my home, and resoundingly registered his displeasure. At one point I remember thinking, *Alright already…I get it!* I really didn't want to see him for a while. (Definition: "a while" = forever.)

Things calmed down, and I felt relatively confident that God had arranged the cosmos to accommodate my need for a break from this gentleman. With my guard sufficiently lowered, I wandered into an informal gathering of friends from the area and…there he was.

My internal prayer meeting only took seconds and it sounded like this: "NO! Not tonight!" And God said, "YES! Tonight! Walk over to him and say, 'Great to see you' and pat him on the knee." This was followed by a very pregnant pause…

When I got over myself, I determined to take a handful of the Kingdom of God with me and I did exactly what God told me to do. When I patted this man's knee he looked up at me like I had just given him a hundred-dollar bill. That's the best way I can describe it. From that moment forward we became friends. A door opened for me to love him and his family over the next several months as I would *never* have dreamed possible before I spoke the Holy Spirit's version of "Peace" to this person on that night.

God wants to raise up an army of believers who carry the timbre of Heaven in their voices so that every word they speak has Heaven's resonance changing the earth. There is to be a transcendent voice in us all that threatens the world with God's catastrophic splendor.

But remember, it is impossible to be cautious and extraordinary at the same time. What disappointment is worthy of your carrying it for another day if it will lock you into a truncated and marginalized vision of God? What failure has you frozen in time in an endless analysis of what went wrong? If you keep focusing on yesterday, you are going to make tomorrow look like your past.

"But I prayed and nothing happened." Nothing happened? Are you sure? Can you see with absolute clarity everything, past, present, and future?

For the sake of argument, let's go with the "nothing happened" conclusion you may be living in. Luke 11:5-13 says that praying is a much larger matter than fixating on a single point of energy. Jesus teaches here that prayer is a passionate pursuit of shameless immodesty. The word "persistence" in verse 8 suggests a "rash-and-without-thought-of-consequence act" that is far from prudent. Think about it for a moment: Are the typical characterizations we hold with regard to prayer related to brazenness, brassiness, imprudence, and shamelessness? I would suggest that most of us view prayer in a completely opposite manner; and this, my friends, is probably why so much of our praying is not changing very many realities on earth.

The story Jesus uses to illustrate His point in the above passage is that of beating on your neighbor's door in the middle of the night to get something to feed unexpected guests. He knows human nature well enough to know that your neighbor will not get up and happily grant your request, but he will get up and give you what you want to make you go away if you have made it clear in your brash attempt to wake him up that you won't go away any other way!

What's the point? Jesus is telling us to treat prayer (and in particular the Lord's Prayer) with this kind of bold brassiness. Get over yourself. Go ahead, knock, and while you're at it, knock loudly because everyone in the house might be asleep. In fact, some ancient liturgical writings of the church preface the Lord's Prayer with these words: "Therefore, let us boldly pray...."

Then Jesus takes this teaching even further into the deep end! He says, *"For everyone who asks, receives; and he who seeks, finds; and to him who knocks* [loudly], *it will be opened."* This is almost scandalous! *Everyone* who asks receives? Everyone, that is, who rises from and rejects their

self-conscious state of prudent, docile, mild-mannered re-
ligiosity to seize the bread of destiny for the feeding of a
spiritually starved culture that has arrived at our church
doors in the middle of a dark night!

Everyone receives who will reject their disappointments
and choose to be rapidly reappointed for their dreams. Everyone receives what? Everyone in this category will receive more
and more of the Holy Spirit, which stops us from dictating to
God how He should answer prayer and ultimately molds us
into becoming the answer to our own prayer because we are
wonderfully filled with the Holy Spirit, again and again.

Years ago as a young pastor I was pained by the overwhelming needs of a new family in our church who were also
brand-new believers. The dad was fresh from prison and had
experienced a very real encounter with Christ. He was a car-
penter with a full set of tools but no vehicle to pack them in
for going to a job, much less finding a job. The mom had her
hands full with two seriously hungry babies. My wife, Ginger,
had fed those preschoolers. She wept and watched one night
as they held their plates to their mouths and shoveled the
food in until they choked…they were genuinely that hungry.
That family desperately needed a pick-up truck.

Not coincidentally, I owned a great old pick-up truck.
I loved that truck. Red, V-8 engine, and the best part…
it was paid for. Parallel to the need of this family, my own
little brood was in a financial bind as well. Tax time had
rolled around and we owed about $700 that we simply did
not have. Well, the pick-up was worth about a thousand

dollars and I decided to take the title to the bank and use the truck as collateral.

On the morning I was headed for the bank I tucked the title in the front cover of my Bible and headed out the door. In those days, I started every day with at least an hour of prayer in our church sanctuary. My prayer that morning consisted of reminding God of the aforementioned needs. He spoke to me very clearly that morning. He said, "Throw down your Bible." Thick-headed as I was at the time, I had not made any connections such as what I think some of you reading this are already making.

When I tossed my Bible on the floor, the pick-up title slid out like a card you pick out of a deck for a card trick. He said, "If you will give Me that title by giving your pick-up to that hurting family, I'll take care of your tax bill in a better way than a loan from the bank."

I wanted God to answer my prayers, and God wanted me to *become an answer to prayer.* I will never forget the joy of giving the keys and title of that great old red pick-up to that sweet family. To be honest, I don't remember how God took care of our tax bill, I just know that He did.

I also know that this was one of those lovely moments that added momentum to our eager pursuit of the Transcendence of the Kingdom of God.

Once the Holy Spirit takes over, from this point we learn to stop praying the problems and we start prophesying the solutions!

"Now may the God of hope fill you with all joy and peace in believing, that you may abound in hope by the power of the Holy Spirit" (Rom. 15:13). We warn people not to get their hopes up; all the while here is God being the God of hope and wanting us to be *abounding* in hope with joy and peace in believing. Since God is in a perpetual condition of hope, I say that hope is always a risk worth taking. Notice, however, that this passage makes it clear that you and I cannot hope out of the shallow pool of our own resources.

To abound in hope is only possible by the power of the Holy Spirit. Don't look now, but part of my intention in writing this book is to challenge us all to get recklessly involved with the Holy Spirit. Stop keeping Him at bay. If you do, it's no wonder your hopes are small. Once the Holy Spirit has the invitation, He will ravage our hopelessness and create a wide vista of dreams and visions. He loves to get our hopes as *up* as *up* can possibly get!

Try this on for size: Jesus lived as one man completely fixated on the Transcendent Reality of the Kingdom of God in the face of the One World Government of His day. He never signed a petition against Rome, much less obsessed with its very real evil. *"He went about doing good and healing all who were oppressed by the devil"* (Acts 10:38), and today Rome is better known for being the headquarters of the world's largest church. Good overcame evil (see Rom. 12:21). If it did it once, it can do it again. Sign me up for that team.

Chapter 8

Mud Pie Indigestion

Too much of a good thing is...wonderful!
—Mae West

C.S. Lewis once said:

Our Lord finds our desires not too strong, but too weak. We are half-hearted creatures, fooling about with drink and sex and ambition when infinite joy is offered us, like an ignorant child who wants to go on making mud pies in a slum because he cannot imagine what is meant by the offer of a holiday at the sea.[1]

In other words, we are far too easily satisfied. We inhale the empty calories of so much artificial stimulation that when reality comes calling, our hunger is ruined. It's like your mom used to say to you about eating before suppertime: "Put that cookie down! It'll ruin your appetite!"

Absolute Goodness and Glory is on the table. The aroma is filling the air and the lions in my spiritual stomach are growling. God has sent the Holy Spirit on a venture of availability, trolling for people who know how to have an honest, heartfelt internal dialogue. *"If I just touch His garments, I will get well"* (Mark 5:28).

Some versions of the story I just referred to describe the event as Jesus perceiving in Himself that "virtue" had just proceeded from Him. The definition of the word *virtue* is "moral excellence and goodness of character." Absolute Goodness trumped temporary badness when someone took the Holy Bait of that Goodness and put a pure-hearted demand on it! Think about this: someone in a crowd seized Jesus' clothes for a brief moment, and that act of a focused appetite became a conduit for Absolute Goodness and Glory to flash into her body sufficient enough to expel and vaporize a 12-year-long sickness.

If you are tired of "making mud pies in a slum," then it's time to set your imagination free to explore what an infusion of God's transcendent Goodness and Glory would materialize if you gave Him just a handful of opportunity.

Right there where you are...through the crowd... through the loneliness...talk to your heart. *Now*...reach, grab, pull it in....

ENDNOTE

1. C.S. Lewis, *Weight of Glory* (1949; repr. HarperCollins, 2001), 26.

Chapter 9

RELEASING THE POWER
OF FORGIVENESS

If you don't live it,
it won't come out of your horn.
—Jazz great, Charlie "Bird" Parker

Right after His resurrection, Jesus "popped" in on the disciples (see John 20:21-23). I like to think of it as something of a playful moment on His part, in some measure simply to leave a lasting impression of what He was about to say to them. Wouldn't you if you could?

John records that Jesus breathed on the group and said, *"Receive the Holy Spirit. If you forgive the sins of any, their sins have been forgiven them; if you retain the sins of any, they have been retained"* (John 20:22-23).

I have no interest in the doctrinal debate that can swirl around any of the words of Jesus. Quite frankly, I don't think Jesus had any interest in that sort of debate either. He came to give us Life, not doctrinal statements. Here I believe He was laying a principle of Life in these pregnant words. He was daring all of us to search out the Life inherent in this principle.

Receive the Spirit and release forgiveness. To me, this is more than learning about how to deal with someone who hurt my feelings, which in turn requires me to forgive them. This is about a much larger picture of what is loaded into this scene.

A recently butchered man is now alive again! He has just passed through a locked door. His body still bears scars and His first words are, *"Peace be with you,"* followed by the above quote from John 20:22-23. Jesus clearly wants His statement to have a lasting and profound impact!

Here's what I believe that impact should be: Get loaded with the reality of the Holy Spirit and then blast the world with spiritual shock waves of forgiveness. Walk through marketplaces and intentionally "ooze" forgiveness, especially when you see someone who is easy to prejudge by appearances. Aim the divine power of forgiveness at every cultural and politically charged issue that comes across your line of sight.

Frankly, I believe that one of the reasons so many people remain incredibly sinful by our own definitions, is that too many of us who call ourselves the people of faith choose to retain sins upon groups we deem either deserving or too guilty of their failures to be helped. We have too rarely given them any other air to breathe around us.

Over the years I have enjoyed several rewarding relationships with a fairly wide variety of people from, how shall I say this tactfully, a broad spectrum of opinions and orientations. What I have discovered is that an old adage about life is profoundly true: people don't care how much you know until they know how much you care. *True forgiveness wins authentic trust.*

I've lost count of the men and women who have crossed my path—from lifestyles widely disdained by the evangelical community—who have trusted my counsel and pastoral care. While I am wholeheartedly "evangelical" because I believe in and live the good news, I have drawn a dark and defining line between me and what many politically motivated evangelicals herald as their core values. And it is not because I necessarily disagree with their values but because I cannot accept their strategies for the spread of their values.

When you live by the sword, you will die by the sword. Today's swords are often political action groups doing legal posturing, demanding our rights and protesting the latest evil on the top ten list. Why do we act like our message has the same root system as everyone else's? Perhaps because it does.

When you live in the Transcendent Supremacy of the Kingdom, you learn that your values are a force of the immaterial, not only capable of withstanding abuse, but ultimately of being alive from a resurrection source.

When I was elected to my first term on a local board of education, the district administrator called me and asked to have coffee. I will never forget his apprehension or his stern demeanor. "Tell me, Reverend. Are you one of these evangelical fundamentalists?" (I learned *after* the election that the year I ran for office was a year that some Christian groups had called for "stealth" candidates to run for school boards. They were encouraged to keep their faith under the radar until after the election and, if they won, to let their secret out and start in on the fundamentalists' agenda.)

I love the Holy Spirit and His genius. Without knowing about any of the political intrigue, I opened my mouth, and through me the Holy Spirit said, "First tell me what you mean by, 'evangelical fundamentalist,' and then I'll tell you if that is what I am."

He proceeded to give me the sad descriptor of what an outside world is often given to expect from us when the power of transcendent forgiveness is not in full operation from our hearts. The laundry list was a sad indictment of "evangelical" fears and paranoia—things that far too many of us have signed petitions for or against and, consequently, too often, advertise our spirit of unforgiveness. (By the way, the word *evangelical* holds a root word, right in the middle: "angel." We are to be like angels with outrageously good news! How did we lose our identity? Well, anyway....)

When he finished, I assured him that I was not one of those people. I told him that my goal in running for school board was to serve the students and families of our district and to do my part to make our children and staff successful.

Many years later, when this good and faithful administrator retired, he sent me a handwritten note thanking me for being a "good and faithful servant" to the community. What was and is my agenda? Releasing forgiveness into an atmosphere too often polluted with rigid politics and ruthless attitudes, sometimes unthinkably done in the name of Jesus.

The crippled man lowered through the roof in the Gospel of Mark had not spoken a word, but Jesus started the conversation by telling him that his sins were forgiven. The woman caught in the act of adultery and brutally dragged to Jesus had not whispered a word of repentance when Jesus took charge of the situation with the anointing to forgive her. The butchers standing around the cross were likely barely coherent due to their vile task, but Jesus spoke to the mountain of their sin and commanded forgiveness upon them.

So, what would Jesus do with the next political petition against a group of people that we are asked to sign? What would Jesus do with the next anybody "caught in the act" and taken to the town square of the evening news? What would Jesus ask us to release with every footstep we take protesting abortion on one side of the political spectrum or war on the other?

Let me help you. He would breathe on us and command us to be genuinely, radically, ridiculously, and uproariously filled with the Holy Spirit so that we could become clouds filled with the water of Heaven's forgiveness! Forgiveness, in this context, is an atmospheric swing, an environmental energy, and a transcendent domain placed within our charge.

Has the power of sin in our day and time taken deep root due, at least in part, to the fact that we, the owners of the franchise of forgiveness, have decided to retain the sins of people who are repulsive to us? Have we become so fortressed against "them" that our radiance is solely for our own illumination inside our comfortable bushel?

When the most easily defined "sinner" puts his or her hand into the communion trays that we pass at our church, I believe that the Kingdom of God is *at hand* for them. I will not refuse that opportunity to anyone, for to do so is to assist in the retention of his sin! Interestingly enough, when Judas reached for the bread and wine at the last supper, he had one more opportunity for the transcendent power of forgiveness to change him. Unfortunately for him, he retained sin by his own choice, failing to recognize the transcendent moment that was alive at his fingertips. Regardless, Jesus did not withhold the opportunity.

The petitions we sign should only be ones that say: "We, the undersigned, petition together to loose a world-changing shock wave of forgiveness upon our nation. Whosoever will, let them come to the Kingdom of God's irresistible influence of freedom through forgiveness. *As it is* in Heaven, you are washed, you are clean, you are covered in the blood of the Lamb, slain from the foundations of the earth; so let it be *on earth.*"

Chapter 10

US WITH GOD...OR GOD WITH *US*?

Too many Christians believe that
Christ came to take us to Heaven.
He didn't. He came to bring the new creation.
—Bishop Kenneth Myers

My chapter title here is too important to give passing notice. You really must pause and read it. Now, which is it? Be careful...this is a trick question. The trick is to get all of us asking ourselves some tough and overdue questions.

The Christmas story teaches us that the angel told Joseph that his new son, Jesus, would be called, "Emmanuel." More than the most common name of a Lutheran church, this title tells us the depths of God's thoughts and character for what He intends to be an unbending reality of our faith. God...*with*...us. *God*...with...*us*. However, in more ways than I care to count or discuss, we have both unintentionally and intentionally distorted that most basic of all truths and have literally reversed it: Us…with God.

After all, we often tell people that the ultimate goal of "getting saved," being confirmed, "praying the sinner's prayer," finishing catechism classes, believing the Four Spiritual Laws, receiving Jesus, etc., is that we "go to Heaven when we die." Hence, "us with God" is the goal. If we are not careful, and I might add, we have not been careful, this ideal becomes "true north" on our spiritual compass. Hence, I believe that we have lost our way (pun fully intended).

Problem is, everything about Jesus, His Life, and teachings, was anchored in the prophetic power of the Emmanuel reality. God stepped into and became *The Human*. The Human did not become a god. The Human did not achieve divinity.

Divinity, if you will, achieved *humanity*. God dignified the human condition and forever made a statement about His goals "down here." Even when we imply subtle changes to that order, we vary from the path like a car drifting over the yellow line on one side or into the ditch on the other side.

God with us means transcendent realities are part of the everyday life of the folks with whom God *is*. God with us means no more being afraid or tired of "this old world." In fact, it means "this old world" should be put on notice that world changers are on the scene. God with us means we are carriers of an insuperable, irrepressible Presence. God with us means that Jesus meant every little word of His prayer, "*...on earth*, as it is in heaven...." And every word of His other prayer, *"...they are not of the world, even as I am not of the world. I do not ask You to take them out of the world, but to keep them from the evil one"* (John 17:14-15).

God with us means we can shred the barrier between us and Heaven and expect heavenly realities breaking out in ever increasing measures in us and around us.

"GOD WITH US" changes everything, and *nothing* about that should be *anything* less than the "true north" on our compass.

I've mentioned Zechariah 8:23 before and I'll refer to it again and again. It promises us that ten people will take us by the shirtsleeve and beg, *"Let us go with you, for we have heard that **God is with you**."* The Radiance of God's reality *with us* must become our obsession! In another passage, the very last words of the Book of Ezekiel (go ahead, look it up!) say, *"...and the name of the city from that day shall be, 'The Lord is there.'"*

Humor me for a moment and reverse that order:

"Oh please take us with you for we have heard,

...That when you die you will go to be with God...

...When the antichrist appears you will go to be with God...

...When you go to church, you go to be with God."

Get the picture? The Emmanuel potential is the genius of the Spirit. Laws of separation of church and state are no match for God with us. A God-less world changes the exact instant that you or I show up.

My goal is not getting to Heaven. My goal is getting Heaven to earth.

The next chapter is an inspiration based on a true story for how to make that happen....

Chapter 11

LET'S MAKE A MIRACLE

S he wasn't supposed to be teaching public school at the age of 57. At least that was her goal 30 years ago. "The Plan" was to take early retirement at 55, move to the Florida Keys, and get a perma-tan. "The Plan" was gone. Its exit began seven years ago when her husband came home with a strange gray look on his face.

He had just learned that his business partner of 16 years had been secretly sabotaging the accounts of their small but successful plumbing business. In a matter of days, the revelation of the partner's long-term gambling addiction erased years of hard work and a lifelong friendship. Bankruptcy was the only way out.

He continued to do the only thing he knew to do, plumbing. Side jobs and the occasional new home project kept him busy. But the bankruptcy and his own integrity did not erase a fairly sizeable amount of debt that he simply chose to pay. And they both agreed that God would always receive the first ten cents of every dollar they earned. The tithe was and would always be holy to God and them.

Now, on this first day of school, the hallways were buzzing with excitement in direct contrast to her bleak mood. She was not supposed to be teaching at the age of 57! But, here she was, going through the motions, decorating the room, dusting off her lesson plans, and pretending to be interested in the fresh new faces entering her second grade classroom. "If I am this emotionally drained today, what will I be in the dead of winter!?" she complained to herself as she called the names of her new students.

"Michael Mayes…Michael Mayes…? Michael? If you are here, please answer!" From the left corner a muttering weak voice said, "Here." Her mind said, "Ugh. I can smell a problem," but the Holy Spirit said, "Look at him. Now! Make eye contact." She knew to be obedient even in the midst of her weariness, and so, looking up and pausing, she gazed at the boy with the weak voice.

From head to toe, his appearance shouted, "I'm tired and I don't want to be here. Leave me alone." Her computer printout indicated that Michael was new to the school, which meant that whatever problems he brought with him would be new as well. The Holy Spirit picked up where He left off: "He's one of the reasons you are back here again. Let's make a miracle together."

Her internal dialogue with the Holy Spirit took milliseconds, but the content was rich with revelation.

"You're hysterical! Here I am sucking my thumb clear up to my elbow and you want to 'make a miracle' with me for this little boy." Woven into the conversation was a rec-ollection of her pastor's recent sermon, "As you go, preach, saying, 'the Kingdom of heaven is within your reach. Heal the sick, raise the dead, cleanse the lepers, cast out demons. Freely you have received, freely give.'" The Spirit closed the exchange with a verbal kiss, "I love you, oh mighty woman of faith and power."

A smile broke across her face like a summer sunrise. "Good morning, Michael." She paused; he shuffled. Under her breath, she whispered, "Thy Kingdom come. Thy will be done, in Michael, just as it is being done in Heaven." Suddenly, he looked back at her, directly in her eyes. It was as if she had thrown a water balloon at him. The Kingdom of the Eternal had just slipped into the moment. Darkness was fleeing at the speed of light and something dead in this little boy was stirring back to life.

A miracle was already made. An empty, wounded teacher became a Kingdom warrior in the blink of an eye.

Chapter 12

REALITY FAITH

Faith is…letting your heart hold a possibility
in the face of multiple disappointments.
—Randy Dean

Recently, someone very dear to me asked me for a way to help a friend to understand faith. My email response was this: "Defining faith to anyone is like explaining love to a junior high kid. It's elusive. It's not a feeling but it does have feelings. It's not a bolt of lightning, but it can produce a 'moment' when the moment is needed. Faith is allowing yourself the privilege of seeing the unseen, reaching for the unreachable, and letting your heart hold a possibility in the face of multiple disappointments." I must say I was pleased with what jumped out of my heart and onto the keyboard. It was without premeditation and dripping with my own passions.

After I read what I had written, it hit me: I needed that definition for myself. If I'm not diligent, I can allow myself the subtle error of thinking that I am a "professional person of faith." No such thing exists in this very real world. Faith must never become canned, packaged, and reduced to formulas. In fact, at that level, it ceases to be faith. We pastors have an occupational hazard of sermonizing life instead of passionately living a life that, in itself, is a message.

Jesus responded to a variety of expressions of faith. In one case a brokenhearted woman wept at His feet and washed His feet with her tears. He called that action "faith," and His response to her tells me that faith is more "felt than tell't." He was not looking for a precise, antiseptic, robotic regurgitation of a memorized lesson. He was looking for the heart. In fact, one of the most quoted Scriptures used to "get people saved" is Romans 10:9-10.

Look closely at this passage. It is crying out for the full engagement of the heart to the power of the resurrection of Christ! *"Believe in your heart that God raised Him...."* Oh, man...that lights a fire in me just typing the words!

"Letting your heart hold a possibility in the face of multiple disappointments...." I believe it was John Wimber who said, "Faith is spelled R-I-S-K." It's about putting your heart "out there" one more time. More and more, I've been putting my heart and my faith right "out there" on my sleeve. Quite frankly, there are moments when it's terrifying...what if nothing happens?

I would rather fail at attempting the miraculous than to succeed at mediocrity.

In the middle of a small prayer gathering where the focus was on a sweet young couple, I heard God say, "One of them has a physical problem with their hearing. Go after it." Even though it was a bit off subject, I asked if either of them had any hearing problems. With a gentle shrug they both said no. A lady off to the side said, "That's for me," and then another lady said, "Me too." That being said, we prayed for the two ladies and the moment passed. I'll admit, I felt a tiny bit foolish, but *I would rather fail at attempting the miraculous than to succeed at mediocrity.* Mission accomplished.

When we finished, the young man who had said he had no hearing problems turned around and with a look of surprise said, "When you prayed for these other ladies, I suddenly became aware of sounds on the other side of the room! Apparently, I had some kind of hearing impairment that I wasn't aware of...my hearing is about 20 percent improved!"

TOO MUCH FAITH?

I'd rather risk the potential foolishness of too much faith than to live the tragedy of a life lived by my own strength and resource. Only the mediocre are always at their best because they never risk anything; they rarely try something new, and they believe only in what they can see, feel, and hear for themselves.

It is a telling commentary that almost everyone believes in the inherent power of evil to spread its influence, but few believe the same about the transcendent power of Goodness to infect, infiltrate, and permeate its surroundings. Don't believe me? The next time someone sneezes on an elevator ask yourself what the following few minutes feel like for everyone trapped in that box. Or take a quick inventory of your faith after you read about or hear of another shooting in a tough neighborhood.

The uproariously good news of the Kingdom of God, as it is displayed and purely taught by Jesus Christ, stands waiting for a company of renewed minds to take it at its core value and conquer nations with righteousness, peace, and joy by the regeneration influence of the Holy Spirit. The potential spread of Absolute Goodness and Glory is far greater through us than any seed of evil ever dreamed of being.

For this, we *must* risk the foolishness of too much faith. For this, someone somewhere must inspire at least a few every day. Do not wait for extraordinary opportunities, but seize the common and ordinary to put an extraordinary God on display...*today!*

Proceed With Caution: Old Man Dreaming Ahead

Joel 2 says that when the Holy Spirit gets His way, even old men have dreams. I used to read that and think in strict categorical terms: Young men get visions…check. Old men get dreams…check. I hope you get the point. I couldn't have been more wrong.

Several months ago another youth camp I ministered to had as its theme, "Dream—Why Not?" It was an awesome time of releasing these students to be free to *see*. Old Testament prophets were sometimes called "seers," because they had a transcendent capacity to look into the heavens and see God's resources and call them down to the earth. Today, Holy Spirit dreaming is seeing "on earth as it is in Heaven."

Joel 2 also says that when the Spirit is truly falling on us that our sons and daughters *can see* and they prophesy! The students at this camp ended up in a torrential outpouring of dreams! It was Psalm 126:1 coming to pass: *"When the Lord brought back the captive ones…we were like those who dream."*

Follow me carefully now: I was the "old man" at that camp. They were the sons and daughters. I prophesied; they dreamed. That's not categorical…it's a transcending weaving in and out and back and forth as the Spirit is allowed to get *big*. I liken it this way: As the Spirit rises in us, He drives our cynical, wooden, rigidity up and out.

You know it's the outrageous power of the Holy Spirit at work when the most likely people among us to be injured by disappointments and frustration (the old) are set free of their unholy fixation on the glorious past and the miserable present *and now they dream!* Remember how we started this chapter? "Faith is allowing yourself the privilege of seeing the unseen, reaching for the unreachable, and letting your heart hold a possibility in the face of multiple disappointments."

Another Kingdom principle we witnessed during that youth camp is hidden in this Joel 2 treasure chest as well. An old man dreamed out loud, and that released sons and daughters to prophesy! How many times have we heard the old song and dance, "What's wrong with kids these days?" I'll tell you what's wrong with them—the older generation keeps holding the Holy Spirit in check and the dreams we ought to be releasing for the healing of our sons and daughters are cheating them of their Kingdom inheritance.

I witnessed it firsthand in that week of camp. Once the spiritual air around these students was cleared with the Word of an old man dreaming, these youth could *see* and became *seers*. When I prophesied, they dreamed; when I dreamed, they prophesied; and the Holy Spirit lived His character among us: *"Where the Spirit of the Lord is, there is liberty."*

Last summer in a Wednesday evening service I was compelled by the Spirit to prophesy that summer was to be the summer of America's Awakening. Sometimes prophecy is a confirming tool and sometimes prophecy is a "make it happen" sledgehammer. I am wielding the latter. Take caution around me these days; I'm in a mood. My dreams are overwhelming me; my eyes have seen the glory. Whether you be young or old and your vision is wilted, I release upon you *now* an all-out attack of the Holy Spirit.

Here's an irony in this mix. I fought some kind of sickness all week at the camp I just mentioned. A cold, allergies, sinus infection...whatever it was, I was physically miserable. Once at home I had the opportunity to call my doctor and, as it turned out, I had an infection known as "pink eye."

Hmm, do you think there's an analogy here? Is it possible that the prince of darkness (yet another impediment to seeing) knew that he must distract an old man in his divine assignment to impart vision to a new generation?

Now, where did I put my sledgehammer....

Chapter 13

IF NOT HERE, WHERE?
IF NOT US, WHO?
IF NOT NOW, WHEN?

When Jesus announced the beginning of His ministry, He said, "The wait is over. God's strategic plan is finally, once and for all, in place. The pervasive and pervading quality of God's perfect authority, command, and domain is within everyone's reach. Change all your previous thinking about what constitutes 'religion' and believe in this announcement of perfect wholeness for all humankind." While this wording may not be familiar to you, it is the RDV of Mark 1:15. I love the RDV. In fact, it's my favorite translation. It speaks from and to the heart—*my* heart, that is. It's the Randy Dean Version as revealed by the Spirit of Truth.

The last time this perfect and pervasive influence had been present on earth was at the creation. God and humans were at complete harmony with each other. Health, wholeness, happiness, artistic creativity, breathtaking beauty, and true human potential were unlimited. Man opted out of that plan, and chaos, disease, and tragic limitations followed. But, because God is infinitely good beyond all definitions, He already had in place a long-range plan for the restoration of His creation. That plan found its new genesis in the aforementioned arrival of Jesus, the Christ.

God's desire for humans to own and manage planet Earth has never been rescinded, but it awaited the arrival of the next Man, or Son of Man, to kick-start the plan all over again. Hence, the announcement Jesus made. From that announcing point forward, Jesus set out to prove His claim. He took control, or dominion, over the chaos, disease, and tragic limitations that the first man had chosen.

If someone was blind, Jesus said, "Here's a taste of God's original plan: *See!*" If someone was dead, Jesus said, "God never planned for death to be the 'norm' on earth. *Live!*" If a party needed wine, Jesus said, "OK. This pushes the limits just a bit, but I'm game. Hey water…let's *party!*" Millions of dollars of lotto money are wasting away in banks all over America. Why? Because hundreds of winners have failed to claim their prizes. It's true. Prizes great and small have been neglected because many people have simply forgotten that they had a lotto ticket or they just tossed the numbers aside, thinking, *What's the use. I'll never win anything.* Similarly, a prize beyond measure has been "buried" in the field of the earth.

Jesus said that the pervading and pervasive influence of God's domain was and is *back*. He also tantalizingly said (in Matthew 13:44-46) that it had been "buried" as a dare for someone somewhere to sell everything they have in order to go buy that field and unearth the treasure.

Too many elements of God's Church today are starving, spiritually bankrupt, and totally ineffective; when the truth is, they are wealthy beyond imagination. They could be a city placed on a hill, the light of the world with the nations streaming to them, happily begging for their tangible Good and the Living God. But sadly, many are just resigned to an insignificant holding pattern, waiting for their number to be called so they can leave the planet that was assigned to their charge.

I don't want to go anywhere until I've finished my desperate search. Along the path of my life, I have worn out three or four shovels digging for that buried treasure I mentioned earlier. Just recently, however, my newest shovel went into the dirt and I felt a sudden "thud." Moments later I was weeping over an open Heaven that I found just beneath my feet. With this discovery in hand, I'd like to invite you to join me at the local expression of the church I pastor. I'm throwing a wedding feast for my portion of the Bride of Christ, and the Groom is in the back room contemplating what to do with several water pots at His disposal.

I don't know about you, but that just makes me want to have a Holy Party!

Chapter 14

"UNARMED TRUTH AND UNCONDITIONAL LOVE"

I believe that unarmed truth and unconditional love
will have the final word in reality.
—Martin Luther King Jr.

I could write the book, *The Idiot's Guide for Coming to Christ.* No choir singing, "Just As I Am," and no counselors waiting with nice smiles and clever Gospel tracts in hand. No heads were bowed, no eyes were closed, no seeker-sensitive "bait and switch" set up to lure me in. I hated church, I hated Christians, and I hated their thinly veiled attempts to witness to me. I hated my mom and dad's new "faith." I hated life and I especially hated me. Hate: pure, raw, real.

Just as I was? I was just between drinking binges at 16. Too cowardly to shoot myself or slice my wrists. But not too cowardly to drive my dad's Cadillac up a hill at 100 miles an hour on the wrong side of the road just to hear my carload of friends scream for mercy and curse me. I will always wonder who it was I almost killed in the other car at the top of that hill. I took the left-hand ditch at the last moment.

The beginning of the end came one night when, in the black cloud of my misery, I was running my head into the walls of my bedroom. That's right, I was literally ramming my skull as hard as I could into the walls hoping to cause an injury bad enough to kill me. (Thirty-seven years later, people close to me now say that might explain some things about me.)

My insanity was based in the lie I had internally authorized and was speaking out between thumps on the wall: "Nobody loves me." I fell asleep, or more accurately, slipped into unconsciousness that night, sobbing those words into my pillow.

I think it was the next day that an old German man from a church my parents were attending came to the house. He parked his old Volvo a block away because he knew I knew his car and would not come home if I saw it parked in our driveway. He sat and waited patiently for me to come home that night because he told my mother he had a dream about me the night before. He didn't tell her what it was. When I walked in the door and saw him sitting in my house, I cursed under my breath....

With a thick German accent he said, "Sit down." Honestly, my knees buckled and I sat. He choked with emotion and continued, "I had a dream about you last night. I saw you crying and saying, 'Nobody loves me.' And God told me to come here tonight and tell you that He loves you and I love you."

I was transfixed. I thought for a moment that I was leaving my body. I remember telling myself to *breathe, don't pass out, and whatever else…don't cry!* I could not speak. I watched helplessly as he came across the room, laid hands on me, anointed me with oil, and left me to ponder what had just happened. I did not pray a sinner's prayer that night…or any night, for that matter. But I knew *something* happened that was not going to go away.

There was a Radiance in that room, and I have spent my life from that moment till this running toward and leaping into the arms of that Radiant God.

More importantly still, all of the above was written to lead to this moment for everyone reading this right now. Gather yourself for a moment of clarity and focus and drink these transcendent words into your soul….

God says to you right now, in this crease of eternity, "My child, I love you." He told me to tell you that. Yes, He did. Whoever you are and whenever you read this, God is looking back at you and speaking those words into your reality. Heaven is merging with you, and you are being irresistibly seized.

God says, "You there, reading this page—I love you." Now put the book down for a moment and bask in His Radiance in the place you are sitting right now.

Long ago, before Christendom began a habit of over-using the term "born again," being "saved" meant something far more transcendent. In his book, *The Relentless Tenderness of Jesus*, Brennan Manning says, "A century ago…in the deep south…the words used to describe the breakthrough into a personal relationship with Jesus were, 'I was seized by the power of a great affection.'"[1]

I am being obedient to a heavenly vision to use this venue to say that we all need to be seized again and again for the restoration of an authentic faith and a Radiant Life. In too many ways, Christianity today has become a system, a "thing," and it does not seize lives as it could and should. That could change, even in this very moment…. There it is again…can you hear it?

His Voice.

LOVE'S ABSOLUTE

His Voice changes everything; and if not everything, then nothing has changed. Whatever isn't changing is likely dying. The key to being part of a change that isn't just changing for change's sake is being changed by something Absolute.

Radical Islamic fundamentalists want change too, but their brand of change is death to the infidels, and well, I guess they don't mind dying, too…which is a teleology that pretty much leaves us all dead. My point is that change has to grow out of a deeper transcending Truth.

Here's what I believe: If you will give God a handful of change, He will give you an acre of Life. God is the only One who can change everything instantly, but He won't impose change where we don't invite it. Hence, giving Him the handful…. You and I don't have to change everything today, but we do need to change something.

So give God one thing about you to love: a simple handful of you. Love changes everything, but first it must love something. One handful is all it takes to start. This real Love is a perpetually expanding and enlarging experience. All this real Love needs is the slightest connection to eventually yeast the entire loaf.

Loved people are extraordinarily and daily changed. You might wish I would tell you that you should reach for a love less transcendent and more like the love of everyone around you. Don't get me wrong, I enjoy loving and being loved by my wife, family, church, and friends. It's just that I have discovered that even if those factors are in place, I am still looking for Love…and Love's Absolute is God.

Too often when we approach the subject of the Love of God, we smile it off with a warm feeling (at best). At worst, it hits an empty detached wish for an experience. Jesus and Paul prayed for something dramatically different: Read John 17 and Ephesians 3:14-19.

Talk about absolute!! Jesus wants us to have the same Love that the Father had for Him from the beginning, when They lived in the mystery of the Trinity…that Holy

Community of Absolute One, though Three. What held them together? Love. And that Love, Jesus prayed, would be ours. Do you believe Jesus always gets His prayers answered? If you do, and you should, you should be expecting an absolute blitz of amazing Love reconstituting your existence!

And Paul gets even crazier because he prayed that we would actually experience God's Love so much so that we would be filled *with all* the *fullness* of God! Recently, in a conference I was speaking to, I suggested that this verse was in fact true and that we need to actualize this Transcendent Reality through whatever means necessary. After the service a dear lady tried to nicely disagree with me by saying, "Oh, if such a thing were to happen, we just couldn't take it. It's just too much." I couldn't respond in the moment without hurting her unmercifully. Why? Because her response typifies too much of our marginalization of so much of the transcendent beauties of God's Kingdom. In doing so we treat God like a bottle of drugs that needs an "accidental overdose" warning on the label.

First John 4:16-19 says, *"God is love...."* God doesn't just love; He *is* Love. This sets an arresting baseline for *all* of our dealings, all of our vision, and all of our pursuit of God. This passage also says that this Perfect Love violently, forcefully, and furiously casts out fear and every related anecdotal deviation even remotely resembling fear.

This kind of Love will ruin us. (In the words that follow, watch my intentional use of the capital letter "L" to represent the Love of God.) Sick, dysfunctional, manipulative posers of love won't stand a chance. The human condition is uniquely vulnerable because God created us to be loved and not just loved. In absence of Love, we become reckless. In the aberrations of Love, we become abnormal. But in the full-on Transcendent Supremacy of God's Love, we are free to become the full-on humans we were all destined to be.

So whether you have put yourself in the vortex of this Love for years or you have not at all, in either case, dive in *now!* I know that some of you want to know how, but the truth is, if I knew how with Western scientific precision, I'd borrow all the money I could and advertise it everywhere I could buy the time and space to shout it out. Why? Because something has to change!

The value of any person, place, or thing is in direct proportion to the Love that is allowed into, on, and through that person, place, or thing. Allow it. Make room for it. Get out of your own way. Get on your knees and accept it. Go out in the woods and open wide your mind and heart to receive it. Just do something to *allow it!*

Jude 20-21 says to keep yourself in the Love of God.

"ARGGGGHHH!" you say. "Tell me how!" But I am telling you that I believe that is part of our problem in the Church today!! We keep crafting multimedia presentations for the consumer-savvy crowds. We do our level best to put the Love of God in a nicely designed witness track so people can make a decision that looks more like a business transaction than an act of passionate response. I refuse to reduce this to a "how to." I can only tell you *why*:

Because this LOVE CHANGES EVERYTHING! It flies into our craving hearts, devastates the plastic idols, and melts our hard, protective walls. His Love consumes and ravages us. When it (He) is truly ours, we are no longer ours.

Fall to your knees *now* and cry out, *"Love me, O mighty God!"*

And He is....

ENDNOTE

1. Brennan Manning, *Relentless Tenderness of Jesus* (Grand Rapids, MI: Fleming H. Revell), 42.

Chapter 15

Hello, My Name Is Truth

*Truth will die with every intention
of living larger, later.*
—Randy Dean

Truth will wreck you. It will set you right-side up in an upside-down world. Truth will strip you of every selfish notion devised by your past, your pains, your problems, your personality, your preferences, your possessiveness, your poverty, your personality, your prosperity, your pity, your power, your perfectionism, your performance, your peers, your paralysis, your predisposi-tions, your prudishness, your put-ons, your papa, and your paranoia.

Truth will meet you head-on with no intention of slow-ing down or dodging you. Its reality will be like headlights frozen on high-beam bearing down on you in its own lane, challenging you to awaken to the reality that you are in the wrong lane. As a matter of fact, Truth won't even honk. That sound you hear is your own adrenalized heart beating.

Truth, while not forgiving in itself, will lead you to forgiveness. Truth is a living power, a driving rainstorm, a relentless blizzard, and a sunshine-drenched perfect day. Jesus said, "I AM the Truth…." Truth walks. Truth talks. Truth laughs. Truth weeps. Truth bleeds. Truth will die with every intention of living larger later.

Truth will set you free, not in spite of these things, but *because* of these things. Truth heals us when we accept the stark fact that we don't know it. Truth delivers us when we crawl across the gravel of life, reach our bleeding fingers toward its hem, and snatch it hard to our weeping face and say in our heart, "If I can just touch the edge of Truth, I will be free."

"I Just Feel So Dry"

My spiritual journey has taken me through a wide range of lessons, emotions, and ultimately, sweet, sweet growth. This book is an extension of my effort to relate what's been entrusted to me; and if you'll have it, make it yours.

Submission to someone who has gained wisdom from God will save years, even decades, for the recipient. Watchman Nee once said, in essence, we can lengthen our lives by buying the years of someone whose spiritual authority is authentic. If that doesn't sound humble enough for you, then I offer this; I've always seen myself as one of God's crash-test dummies. If you just long to be thrown into walls and spend your time picking up the pieces, then go ahead…you can quite literally knock yourself out. Or, I offer you my test results.

As you can see from the lead in to this chapter, I see Truth from a transcendent perspective. It transcends words, it exceeds thinking, and it is a force of God's Nature to contend with or surrender to. Someone once said, "The truth will set you free, but first it will make you miserable." The length of the season of misery is entirely up to us. If we resist it, if we try to negotiate with it, and even if we acknowledge it but postpone our cooperation with it until a more convenient time, the misery is ours and the freedom waits.

Here's a truth: Psalm 68:5-6 says, *"A father of the fatherless and a judge for the widows, is God in His holy habitation. God makes a home for the lonely; He leads out the prisoners into prosperity, only the rebellious dwell in a parched land."* The Amplified Version of verse 6 says, *"God places the solitary in families…."*

Note the clear description of God's character, which anchors Him in His purposes, plans, and procedures. Everything God does flows out of His enthroned character. Since He is a perfect Father, He acts in our lives *as* a father to shepherd us into families and out of solitude. When He sees loneliness, He acts precipitously to create a home, a covering, and a protective, productive environment to drive the loneliness far from our experience. Why? To create the hothouse for our best human potential.

Even if I have done something worthy of imprisonment, God is acting just outside my line of sight arranging a scenario for my prosperity if I will dare to cooperate. I can most certainly choose to throw in the towel and spend my remaining days crying about how "the man" put me down, and I will most certainly die with an impoverished heart. Or I can come out of whatever prison I've been in, lean hard on the enthroned character of God, and discover new treasure and prosperity for my soul.

But it's the last part of Psalm 68:6 that can really shake us up: *"…only the rebellious dwell in a parched land."* Ouch! Do you see what I see? Since God's character will only allow Him to be Good and out of that Goodness He is creating a home, a covering, and a protective productive environment for my highest and best human potential, then the only thing that could put me in a parched dead place is my own rebellion to Him.

Now here's the punch line of this whole matter: God's Kingdom Transcendence functions at its highest supremacy in the context of the anointed corporate family. That's called covering. When I am in a covering, I am submitted to the greater purposes, plans, and procedures of God's greater power and presence. When I am separate from covering, I am subject to the parched and withering effects of standing alone in the wind and heat. In a covering I am consistently available to the natural and supernatural resources gathered by a family made for me by God's enthroned character.

It's impossible to be dried out in that climate! In fact, another Psalm (133) says that when spiritual siblings dwell (consistently hang together) in unity (passionate purpose), it is like the dew of Hermon coming on the mountains of Zion and God *commands* a blessing there! Where God *commands* blessings, you don't have to ask for blessing.

If I'm parched, then I need to return to the last place I remember being watered. For me, that would be in a Spirit-anointed covering family. But to be perfectly honest, I cannot remember the last time I felt parched…no brag, just fact. Why is that, you might ask? Because I refuse to live outside of the atmosphere of God's character, which is always preparing the environment of a covering home creating the hothouse for my highest and best.

Due to the events I described earlier in this book, my wife Ginger and I have begun a process of traveling to Redding, California, to establish a covering home relationship with Bethel Church. We have spent the past two years looking into what God is doing through Pastor Bill Johnson and the Bethel tribe, reading countless books and articles by them, listening to hundreds of hours of teaching, relating with as many people as we can by phone, face, or computer, and ultimately falling in love with everyone and everything we came in contact with. (Not the least of which is Rich Oliver, pastor of Family Christian Center in Sacramento, California. Rich heads up the ordination arm of the connection to Bethel and has proven to be an apostle, a father, and a gentleman.)

Oh, and lest I forget one important detail...we furiously sought the face of the Father for discernment and leading.

The end result is that our church and Ginger and I are now a part of a Kingdom Family that goes by the name of Global Legacy (the church networking arm of Bethel). We have entered into this covering with more joy than I can adequately express with the English language. I've told many people that the DNA match is perfect, and the atmosphere of Heaven's Kingdom is increasing in us and around us exponentially. The air of our church is tangibly *alive* and spiritually drenched! We're not praying for revival; we are busy having one. The Kingdom of God is present here with power!

Our prayer now is for stewardship of this work to spread through time and space as it is passed to the next generation for multiplication of its efficacy and influence.

The reason we began this search is that, as I described earlier, the family of covering where we had been for 25 years was no longer able to function in that capacity. I will continue to follow the path of the honorable sons of Noah who backed into the bedroom to discreetly cover the embarrassment of their dad (see Gen. 9:23) as it relates to this matter. It is only germane to this subject to say that the time had come for us to follow God's character into this new family.

Here's the specific teachable moment of this point: If you are and have been parched for some definable length of time, ask yourself: "Am I cooperating with the precipitous nature of God's desire to cover me with spiritual family?"

Even if you are physically in a church you might be rebelling against what God is trying to do on your behalf in the context of that tribe. The result is that dry dearth all around you. End the rebellion, and dive into the deep end of what God is doing in your spiritual family.

Or, you might be staying in a church where God has not specifically planted you. Your thirst is calling you out of that wilderness. "Oh, but brother…God has called me to the wilderness." There are two types of wildernesses in Scripture: one was the result of rebellion where a few days' journey turned into 40 years of wandering. If that's your wilderness…for crying out loud *repent* and get out of there! The other wilderness lasted for 40 *days* and ended in a reverberating triumph over the devil when Jesus stepped forward into His destiny.

If your "wilderness" has lasted longer than 40 *days,* your victory over the devil is overdue. Get a Word from God, and put darkness under your feet as you walk out of the wilderness and into your destiny.

It is impossible to be dry for more than a few days at a time if I'm properly positioned in the spiritually covering family that the nature and character of God has drawn me into.

I will paraphrase Psalm 1 to end this chapter: "Blessed are those who have had an awakening of heart, soul, and mind to end relationships that just suck the life out of them without any return or end in sight. They have the Spirit's good sense to be delighted with God's nature and character, which will plant them in river-enriched soil that supernaturally makes them like the most glorious trees you have ever imagined, with leaves as big as elephant ears and greener than Al Gore. Everything they touch flourishes, thrives, and prospers because they are loaded with an intrinsic value that radiates out from them and brings value to their surroundings."

Chapter 16

Soapbox Warrior, Wisdom

Wisdom shouts in the street... (Proverbs 1:20).

The following story grew out of a vision I had of a cosmic street corner and mysterious, metaphorical preacher. This is a clarion call for all of us to find our corner, our soapbox, and our voice of the Spirit. Your corner may be your office cube, your soapbox may be your desk...just be aware that the transcendent nature of the Kingdom Call in our voice can lock on to otherwise unaware passersby with a Heavenly Cry.

A lonely figure wanders to a busy street corner and throws a wooden crate down with a crash. His features are striking, with long, gray hair and piercing, dark eyes. There is nothing noteworthy in his attire, except to say that it is clean, pressed, and simple. With his box in place, he steps upon it and slowly draws a small black book from the back pocket of his jeans. Most people walking by seem determined not to notice the unusual actions of this man who is making it clear that he will soon be attempting to gain a great deal of attention.

The pages of the small black book are worn, even ragged, and his eager search through the book makes it clear why it is in such an abused condition. Suddenly, he sees in the tattered pages what he longed to see, and with a long drawn breath he sharply exhales the words, "Repent, for the Kingdom of Heaven is at hand! Make ready the way of the Lord, make His paths straight!" A few people walking by are startled by the break in the voiceless silence; still others are visibly upset at the intrusive effort made by this stranger. However, two and three, now five and six people inquisitively stop to listen, sensing in the voice a mysterious distant call from somewhere strangely familiar yet sadly undefined.

A large vein swells on the side of this man's neck with every passionate word he speaks. It would appear that this vein would burst from the weight of the words he is pushing into the air of this busy street corner. Still, most passersby want nothing to do with this odd demonstration; they have no interest in the rantings of this voice. But to the half dozen who have stopped, there is a greater urgency in the content of these words than there was just moments ago in their harried and hurried footsteps. Like the swollen vein in his neck, their hearts are beginning to swell from the passion of the words.

The echoes off nearby building walls naturally amplify the voice above the sounds of cars and trucks as he cries out, "We live in a world gone mad with self-promotion, indulgence, and ego. Men find pleasure from their power over a girl. Women seek revenge on males through harsh manners and crude gestures. Babies are torn from the last safe haven on earth by forceps and suction; and children, confused by the insanity, mistakenly act out their rage by brutalizing their peers. Laws and government are powerless to heal. Self-important religious bigotry only parades itself as master of the obvious. There is only one answer! A new heart! And only the God who lovingly fashioned you in the secret place of His almightiness can give you that new heart. Today, let Him slip His invisible hand into your chest. Let Him crush your heart of stone into the powder from which He will then with gentle genius recreate a heart of soft, infant-like quality.

"From that new heart will beat a new rhythm of Life. Birds will sing symphonies without beginning or end. The rain will wash your face, the sun will dry your tears, the moon will dance through the night sky and draw from your eyes a wonder and awe for which you long. Your sins, which stain you like a warrior of hate, will be displaced and removed so that the only thing from this day forward that you will wish to fight will be the old self you once treasured and despised. Come this day to Jesus, for He is your God."

Now, the six who were stopped by a mysterious Power are bowing on the sidewalk, a concrete altar. Their shoulders quiver from the release of long-held emotions. A wide section of this street corner has been allowed to this tiny cathedral gathering as pedestrians pretend to ignore what is all too obvious. The man from the crate steps down and touches each bowed figure with kindness that seems foreign to the volume of his just-finished speech. One by one, those who have been bowed stand tall and look at each other as though they have just each one arrived home from a faraway place. They are inexplicably changed. So too will the world around them be changed as they each go home and find small planks of wood, nails, and a hammer with which to create their own wooden crates.

Holy Beast

This parable I just used describes yet another transcendent "something" I am seeking.

I'm tracking a Holy Beast. His footprints and trail are everywhere around me. It's not so much that He is hiding from me as it is that He is hidden *for* me. In sublime moments here and there I thought we were completely intersected, but He slipped away, or more accurately put, I assumed discovery while He sighed, "That's the porch. I'm in the Great Room."

For three decades I've read two passages of mystery: *"Now when they heard this, they were pierced* [violently stung] *to the heart, and said to Peter and the rest of the apostles, 'Brethren, what shall we do?'"* (Acts 2:37), and *"While Peter was still speaking these words, the Holy Spirit fell* [affectionately seized with a violently grasping embrace] *upon all those who were listening to the message.*

All the…believers…who came with Peter were amazed, because the gift of the Holy Spirit had been poured out…" (Acts 10:44-45). In these brilliant word pictures I see that Peter, perhaps unwittingly, perhaps not, is unlocking the Kingdom of Heaven and Something, quantitative *and* qualitative, drops with an unmistakable thump, and entire gatherings of people are blessedly attacked and desire no escape.

The truest essence of the language in these passages is that these people were seized, grasped, taken hold of, clutched, and clasped; and while it was an affectionate seizure, it was with more or less violence than we might like to think. It was seminal, determining, generative, axiomatic, a point of origin, a fountainhead, a wellspring, a dictum, and a command catalyst.

Western sensibilities long to tame this Holy Beast. Like a circus lion, we want it to play with the tamer, roar only on command, and send me home with giddy arrogance. (Here I am reminded of C.S. Lewis's words from *The Chronicles of Narnia*: "Aslan is not a tame lion.") It offends our rational democratic pleasure of always wanting to take our time, consider the options, and come back later, after we've played the intellectual, to cast a vote against it. Yet, I've come to believe that He is eager to write a new book, *How the West Was Won; Again*.

I'm serious about this. There are Keys of the Kingdom for the unlocking of this undomesticated God, and if Peter could stumble his way into their usefulness, then I refuse to be denied. In her book, *Teaching a Stone to Talk,* Annie Dillard describes my heart perfectly:

> Why do we people in churches seem like cheerful brainless tourists on a packaged tour of the Absolute? On the whole, I do not find Christians, outside of the catacombs, sufficiently sensible of conditions. Does anyone have the foggiest idea what sort of power we so blithely invoke? It is madness to wear ladies' straw hats and velvet hats to church; we should all be wearing crash helmets. Ushers should issue life preservers and signal flares; they should lash us to our pews. For the sleeping god may awake someday and take offense, or the waking god may draw us out to where we can never return.[1]

She quotes a Hasidic rabbi as refusing to visit a friend the next day by explaining, "How can you ask me to make such a promise? This evening I must pray, 'Hear O Israel.' When I say these words, my soul goes out to the utmost rim of life.'"

We are all beckoned to that utmost rim of life, but *in Christ,* to return with the Hurricane Breath of God to unleash an irresistible Word. I've just participated in burying one too many young lives to believe that God does not have an irresistible Answer.

Pardon me, but I think I heard a Roar a few meters from where I'm sitting.... You can stay where it's safe if you'd like, but I'm on my way to be delightfully devoured by a Holy Beast who longs to be found.

WHEN GOD ATTACKS

One night, not long ago, I was getting ready to speak at a Saturday night conference in the Minneapolis/St. Paul area. The band was spiritually and authentically on fire with true and pure worship. I was a wonderful wreck trying to blink through my tears to keep eye contact with the worship leader so I would know when it was my time to preach. Suddenly, and without any personal intention on my part, I was seeing a vision. If that makes you nervous, I cannot help you. It is true, it is lovely, and it happened.

I saw a gigantic icy white lion. Not C.S. Lewis's Lion. At that time, I had not seen the movie version of *The Chronicles of Narnia,* and besides, this vision happened before the fanfare or even the ads for that movie. The lion was ravenous, glorious, and lasered in on me. All at once I heard God's voice saying to me, "Randy, I want to attack your soul!" I do not know how loud I spoke back, but I do know I responded immediately by saying, "Please, come and attack me, now!" The lion blurred directly at my face as I threw my arms wide open. When he came upon me I was bathed in his whiteness. When the icy-colored fog lifted, I looked in my lap. The lion became an enormous, delicate Lamb. I shared the experience that night and the next morning at my home church.

Almost three months later, one of our assistant pastors, Steve, came to me with a book in hand and said, "Pastor, look at the part I highlighted." Here is what I read:

> I will not leave you alone. You are Mine. I know each of My sheep by name. You belong to Me. If you think I am finished with you, if you think I am a small god that you can keep at a safe distance, I will pounce upon you like a roaring lion, tear you to pieces, rip you to shreds, and break every bone in your body. Then I will mend you, cradle you in My arms, and kiss you tenderly.[2]

I am currently basking in this Attack. Outside of God's ravening brilliance, I can faintly hear and see the hell that hates God's work in me. Just beyond the glory of God's hunger for me, I am also vaguely aware of people who don't understand or like what they see God doing to me. Unfortunately for them, they are too terrified to step into the fray to "rescue" me. I say "unfortunately for them," because if they understood this Attack, they would be the rescued and not the rescuers.

An Old Testament man named Jacob wrestled with God and walked funny for the rest of his life. I expect as a New Testament man, I will come out of this Attack a dancing fool for the Lamb of God. *Watch me!* If I've said that once, I've said it a thousand times. *Watch me!*

The Sound of Resurrection

Luke 4:31-37 and 43 is a compelling narrative that is wrapped around the themes of voice, message, and authority. *"And they were amazed at His* [Jesus'] *teaching, for His message was with authority"* (Luke 4:32). Then, Luke accounts that a demon-possessed man cried out with a loud voice, *"Have You come to destroy us? I know who You are— the Holy One of God!"* (Luke 4:34).

This is a peculiar picture…

Notice that the demon does not say anything necessarily bad or wrong. Jesus did come to destroy the works of the devil. Jesus was and is the Holy One of God, but Jesus doesn't want to let this little beast occupy the airwaves any more than the brief moment it grabs. In fact, Jesus puts a Word on him, *"'Be quiet and come out of him!' And when the demon had thrown him down in the midst of the people, he came out of him without doing him any harm"* (Luke 4:35).

Luke says that even more amazement came on the crowd and, *"They began talking with one another saying, 'What is this message? For with authority and power He commands the unclean spirits, and they come out'"* (Luke 4:36).

Let's take some pains to list what we see here:

1. Jesus puts authority in the air. The Greek word for *authority* here means force, liberty, freedom, mastery, capacity, influence, jurisdiction, and

a right to enforce. I would call it a field of Transcendent Supremacy.

2. Demons know church-speak. They love to fill rooms with empty, vacant, lifeless religious sounds. Swearing, drooling, and threatening are simply too obvious.

3. The question pregnant with purpose was, *"What is this message? For with authority and power He commands the unclean spirits, and they come out."*

4. Luke 4:43 answers the above question in the words of Jesus: *"I must preach the kingdom of God...for I was sent for this purpose."*

Psalm 29 says that God's voice thunders and is majestic. It hews out flames of fire, shakes wildernesses, and makes nations skip like frightened calves when we see that He speaks as the King of Infinity. When Jesus spoke He put a new jurisdiction into the atmosphere around Him. His voice was an affidavit and a warrant from Heaven's Kingdom. He put God's jurisdiction in the environment, and even if you did not understand Him, you knew you must hear more.

Remember when Jesus freaked out the well-fed crowd in John 6? *"Truly, truly, I say to you, unless you eat the flesh of the Son of Man and drink His blood, you have no life in yourselves."* Yikes! Talk about a sound bite (pun fully intended) that could be used against you! After the thousands left Jesus to find a better preacher, He told His remaining disciples that if you don't "get" that, you won't "get" what's coming, because, "My words are spirit and are life."

Interestingly enough, their response underscores everything we're looking at: *"Simon Peter answered Him, 'Lord, to whom shall we go? You have words of eternal life'"* (John 6:68). Eternity here is not measured in quantity. This is the quality of transcendence. Another way to say what Peter expressed is, "There's eternity in Your voice."

When Jesus spoke, He put a new jurisdiction into the atmosphere around Him. His voice was an affidavit and a warrant from Heaven's Kingdom. He put God's jurisdiction in the environment, and even if you did not understand Him, you knew you must hear more. Now do you want to read something that will either bless you or freak you out some more? Luke 10:16 says, *"The one who listens to you listens to Me, and the one who rejects you rejects Me...."*

I simply *must* have that Voice! I refuse to fill rooms with vacant religious sounds that leave people unchanged and dominated by the poisons of our culture.

I simply *must* be one whose voice is a carrier of that Voice. I am on this planet to be His warrant officer, the bearer of the King's Jurisdiction that arrests the darkness, puts it out of commission, and fills the atmosphere with "Thy Kingdom come, Thy will be done, on earth, as it is in Heaven."

And I simply *must* find others who cry out for this mantle, this vocal clothing that can be touched, for the healing of those who say in their hearts, "When I touch this, *I am healed!*"

ENDNOTES

1. Anne Dillard, *Teaching a Stone to Talk* (Harper Perennial, 1982), 52-53.

2. Brennan Manning, *Lion and Lamb* (Chosen Books, 1986).

Chapter 17

Metamorphosis

When you find Christ and His Kingdom,
you find yourself.
—E. Stanley Jones

An incredible account is given to us in Matthew 17, Mark 9, and Luke 9 of the Transfiguration of Jesus. I have eagerly poured over this account more times than I can count in my nearly four decades of loving God and His Word. I have tried a few times to bring some kind of adequate teaching as a pastor from this treasure. Commentaries help with some discussion of location, Greek grammar, and lexical assistance, but in the end, they bore me.

My soul cries out for a spirit of wisdom and revelation in the knowledge of Him. What's really here? In Second Peter 1:16-21 the apostle gives us the only personal accounting of this event in a teaching format. For me, this is the only trustworthy commentary. I'll come back to this momentarily.

Romans 12:1-2 urges us to refuse the current cultural mindset, but it doesn't stop with a negative. Paul takes aim at another Mount of Transfiguration for every believer: "...*but be **transformed** by the renewing of your mind....*" Paul revs up the spiritual engine of command and shouts that each one of us needs a regular furnace blast of a *meta* or glorious moment.

The prefix "meta" means over, or beyond. Remember how transcendence is "beyond" or "exceeding"? The Greek word for *transformed* that Paul chose to use is the word "metamorphoo." In biology it would be used to describe how the tadpole becomes the frog. This word that Paul used is the same word used to describe what happened to Jesus on the Mount of Transfiguration. In a moment, we'll splice these accounts together.

But before we proceed too much further, let me speak to the "word of caution" that might be forming in someone's mind—that inevitable concern about experiences and emotionalism. Let's take on experiences first.

Jesus is having an experience right here in the story of the Transfiguration! That ought to be enough to validate such an eventuality in any of our lives. But for the sake of being thorough, let's continue.

His experience is necessary for His state of mind and soul given the fact that Jesus is looking down the barrel of His impending death, and perhaps is feeling very human. Have you ever faced the prospect of a serious medical procedure? Or had some serious life-changing or even life-threatening event hanging in the air before you?

Take that sensation and multiply it by a hundred thousand and maybe you've got an inkling of Jesus' post in life at that time. So, with complete intentionality, to experience His Father and His Father's Heaven, He took Peter, James, and John in tow up the mountain to pray.

Luke's account says that, *"While He was praying, the appearance of His face became different…"* Read all this narrative for yourself, and if you will read it with the Holy Spirit's eyes in your eyes, get ready to find your own mountain. Right now, at this very moment my mountain is right here in my office.

Jesus needed a *meta* experience for the benefits of its metamorphosis. He also knew that Peter, James, and John needed a teachable *meta* moment, so He took them along to fry their circuits.

Will someone possibly abuse what I'm saying here and push into a fraudulent experience possibly confusing others? Of course! But is a lockdown on Christianity required to prevent any and all abuses of God's grace? What *greater abuse* do we perpetuate when we build walls around these matters and potentially rob the Church of a chance *to radiate something from a transcendent source*?

I am reminded of a quote by John Muir, a conservationist, geologist, and naturalist from a century ago, who loved the wilderness. Of the potential risks inherent to the wild he loved he said:

> To the timid traveler, fresh from the sedimentary levels of the lowlands, these highways, however picturesque and grand, seem terribly forbidding—cold, dead, gloomy gashes in the bones of the mountains, and of all Nature's ways the ones to be most cautiously avoided. Yet they are full of the finest and most telling examples of Nature's love; and though hard to travel, none are safer. For they lead through regions that lie far above the ordinary haunts of the devil, and of the pestilence that walks in darkness. True, there are innumerable places where the careless step will be the last step; and a rock falling from the cliffs may crush without warning like lightning from the sky; but what then? Accidents in the mountains are less common than in the lowlands, and these mountain mansions are decent, delightful, even divine, places to die in, compared with the doleful chambers of civilization. Few places in this world are more dangerous than home. Fear not, therefore, to try the mountain-passes. They will kill care, save you from deadly apathy, set you free, and call forth every faculty into vigorous, enthusiastic action. Even the sick should try these so-called dangerous passes, because for every unfortunate they kill, they cure a thousand.[1]

As to the dangers of experiences I am frankly far more concerned about timid lives that fear them. As John Muir just said, "…Few places in this world are more dangerous than home…"

I would rather correct extravagance than prod lethargy.

As to the emotionalism that can easily accompany an experience, look at poor Peter on the mount. "Terrified" is how the New American Standard Bible puts it. From where I'm sitting, it sure looks like God intentionally pushed some emotional buttons in this experience.

To be sure, emotions aren't everything…*but*, they are *something!*

Leonard Sweet says in his book, *The Gospel According to Starbucks*:

> In premodern times and in the Eastern Church, religious experience was not held suspect in the laboratory of reason…How we acceptably expressed our emotions in the modern era without being thought a theological troglodyte was through music… Christians in the West became more interested in beliefs about prayer than prayer experiences…*If Christianity really wanted to get radical, the first thing it could do would be to stop privileging Western rationalism.* [Emphasis mine.][2]

Just for the sake of keeping my composure while I'm writing this, let me draw your attention to the conclusion I promised you earlier by returning to Second Peter.

Peter says of that moment that he isn't trying to sell a philosophical page-turner for the *New York Times* best-seller list. He says, *"We made known to you the power and coming of our Lord Jesus Christ…we were eyewitnesses of His majesty…."* And then he pushes me off the cliff of credulity when he says, *"…we have the prophetic word made more sure to which you do well to pay attention as to a lamp shining in a dark place, until the day dawns and the morning star arises in your hearts."*

"Pay attention as to a lamp shining in a dark place," Peter says. "Run to the Radiance," Randy says. *"…Until the day dawns and morning star arises in your hearts,"* Peter says. "The Transcendent Supremacy of the Kingdom of God is waiting to explode inside of you," Randy says. *Get transfigured….*

"How do I get transfigured," you ask? Find a mountain, seek out a cabin, run to a closet, go to a raucous revival meeting, hide in a motel room, get up in the middle of the night and stand under the stars, find a lit-up Latino church, go to an alive African-American church, come to my church, go to Bethel Church in Redding, California, and whatever you do, *just get UP and DO something.*

The Transfiguration did not come to Jesus; He went after it. Being transformed by the renewing of our minds won't come to you, but Scripture says, *"…present your bodies a living and holy sacrifice…."* **Get UP and DO something.**

I've been telling my church and now you who read this that we need a baptism in Absolute Goodness and Glory

Metamorphosis

if we are to have any credible refutation of the absolute bad and evil that soaks our world. If Jesus needed a metamorphosis in a cloud of glory because He climbed that mountain and prayed into it, we dare do no less for our often-pitiful mindsets.

Jesus said that we are the light of the world, and this little light of mine, baby, I'm gonna *light it up*.

I am arising; I am shining because the glory of the Lord has risen upon me. *Because* deep darkness is upon the people of non-transfiguration, the Lord has risen upon me and His glory is appearing on me, to such an extent that entire nations are seeing it and coming to that light (see Isa. 60).

Let me add this cherry on the top: after the resurrection of Jesus, Matthew records that His appearance, His "fashion," His aspect, the very sight of Him was "like lightning." There is yet another latent potential waiting for you and me.

OK…I'm done talking to you now…I have got to go get me some of that! The world around me has been dying for too long. I've got an assignment.

ENDNOTES

1. John Muir, *The Eight Wilderness Discovery Books* (London: Diadem Books, 1992), 328. Reprinted

153

with permission from *Steep Trails* by John Muir
(Muir-Hanna Trust, 1918), 328.

2. Leonard Sweet, *The Gospel According to Starbucks*
(WaterBrook Press, 2007), 171-173.

Chapter 18

"LET'S TURN TO THE LAST BOOK OF THE BIBLE: REVELATIONS"

*Too often the church leaves a blur
instead of a mark....*
—E. Stanley Jones

Do you see anything wrong with the chapter title? The Bible does not have a book in it called "Revelations." You might say that I am being picky. I can live with that; this is America and you have the right to be wrong.

I am not being picky...what I am being is a shepherd who watches over the flock by night and I have scouted out a sick wolf stalking the flock.

Skinny and mangy, and yet, he is the most hazardous type of wolf to the sheep because he is a wolf of doctrinal purity and theological precision. He can quote ten Scriptures faster than you can say the Pledge of Allegiance or the Lord's Prayer. This wolf has misrepresented the character of God and the beauty of Jesus Christ with impunity through some in Christian media and literature. This wolf believes that the last book of the Bible is a spooky collection of revelations about the (cue the scary organ music, please) "endtimes."

The simplicity of the Book of Revelation is found immediately in its opening verse: *"The Revelation of Jesus Christ, which God gave Him to show His servants—things which must shortly take place."* That simple statement has been mangled, twisted, abused, stretched, ignored, and pluralized.

But what if this book is not at all about the "end of the world" business? What if the book is not at all about a seven-year anger itch that God has buried in His nasty side? What if the opening words really do say it all? A Revelation, completely of Jesus Christ, about things, which must *shortly* take place.

(Side note: if you and I are building a wooden box and you ask me to bring you a short piece of wood, and I show up with a 20-foot length of lumber, what will you say to me? "Shorter, please," right? And if I continue to show up with lengths of lumber that measure between 10 and 19 feet long, my hunch is that you'll give up and go get a short piece of wood for yourself. My point is, when Revelation *opens* with the word "shortly," I don't think we need to dig around at the lumberyard for anything that even resembles "long.")

What if the word pictures, the mysterious images, the mystical portraits and the colors, smells, numbers, scrolls, trumpets, bowls, and beasts are just exactly what the first verse says? What if it is about Jesus Christ and things that have taken place, are taking place, and will always take place in human history? What if Revelation 1:8 lays a perfect grid over the entire book: *"I am the Alpha and the Omega, says the Lord God, who is and who was and who is to come, the Almighty."* Is, was, and is to come; that's at least three dimensional.

What if this majestic book is multidimensional, transcendently exceeding Western sensibilities and required reading only when we, like John, are "in the Spirit on the Lord's day"? And if being, "in the Spirit" is required…

Wouldn't that sick wolf I referred to earlier be determined to "pick off" any Spirit-drenched believer from bringing a pure comprehension to a Revelation of Jesus Christ that would fully unpack the complete majesty and replete glory of who Jesus Christ really is? Wouldn't it be the most complete irony to have people who adore being "in the Spirit on the Lord's day," distracted away from a *Revelation* by having them amused by revelations?

"Amused" is a powerful word. To "muse" is to ponder, deliberate, reflect, and think deeply, over and over again. When you add the prefix "a," for all intents and purposes you unplug whatever follows the prefix. So to be "amused" is to be unplugged from the challenge of thinking deeply.

The dear man who wrote Revelation, John, was a man of poetic eloquence and passionate expression. He had laid his head on the chest of Jesus at the last supper. Throughout his Gospel he referred to himself as the disciple whom Jesus loved. I like to tell people that "Jesus loves you, but I'm His favorite." (You're welcome to borrow that if you'd like; just remember, I'm *still* His favorite.)

This was a man of profound feelings who must have struggled mightily to find words and means to express the unimaginable things revealed to him. God took a magnificent risk in trusting such a soul to write this book, but it was a necessary risk in order to paint the portrait that emerged.

Now then, think of this book as the most majestic original word painting ever created.

It is not a collection of revelations. It is the depth, width, height, and length of a Jesus most of us have never seen. It is an artist's view of history from the perspective of the heavens. We get to climb up on the inside of Jesus Christ, see through His eyes, and contemplate with the engagement of His soul. I liken it to being injected into the bloodstream of Christ. With the help of the Holy Spirit I am traveling in a timeless zone that is rich in metaphors, images, and word pictures. I get to see how all of history is summed up in Christ as Ephesians 1 teaches me.

This spirit journey includes a flight through His emotions, His holy sense of self, and His wildly unselfish sense of humanity. No human has ever walked the earth the way

Jesus walked the planet. His unlimited perceptions of it all and His report back to the Father point to a Jesus Christ who must be discovered by the Church.

I dare you who read this to completely shed yourself of the religious baggage you may have taken on and join me in an animated treasure hunt for the real, one and only Jesus Christ. I believe we have not yet seen and known the Real Jesus because I believe there is cosmic depth of Him that can only be found in the Book of Revelation, once we jettison our tissue-thin views.

I don't recall the details, but years ago I heard of a pastor who got really sick of all the comic book renditions of Revelation and he decided to simply read the Book out loud for himself. The reason he did this was the promise of verse 3 of the first chapter, *Blessed is he who reads and those who hear the words of the prophecy, and heed the things which are written in it; for the time is near.*

Not long after his personal reading, he decided to read it out loud, with zero commentary, to his congregation. The report I heard was that as he finished he looked up and everyone in church that night was on his feet praising God.

I've since done this in my church a number of times, with the same results.

I've seen this principle taken even further. Several years ago I was speaking about the power of the Word at yet another youth camp. One of the leaders came to me on the second day and said, "I've got this strange impression that we are supposed to read the Bible, out loud, in its entirety, during this week at camp." Strange indeed!

He and I both knew that time constraints would be prohibitive to that goal. What we arrived at was this; he divided the Bible into small, bite-sized portions and put the references onto small slips of paper. We then put all those slips of paper in a box, brought them to a meeting of the entire camp (around 200 youth and adults) and told everyone to take out a reading assignment, get a Bible and read the passage on that slip of paper out loud and when they were finished to get another slip, and so on and so on.

What followed was amazing! All through the room there was a growing crescendo of a blended symphony of the Words of God. *"For I received from the Lord that which I also delivered to you, that the Lord Jesus in the night in which He was betrayed took bread..."* was woven into the sound of, *"My son, do not forget my teaching, but let your heart keep my commandments; for length of days and years of life and peace they will add to you...."*

The students couldn't sit still. They were pacing all through the chapel. Their voices were getting stronger and more passionate with every word! The room was alive with a roar that went on for the better part of two hours. High school football players were weeping through the words. Young ladies were laughing the words out! Groups of friends made circles and read a wild cacophony of words from genealogies to Genesis.

When the box of references was empty, we had instructed them to wait until every verse was completed so that we could read the last chapter together in unison from the Book of Revelation.

When we got to verse 19, *"And if anyone takes away from the words of the book of this prophecy, God shall take away his part from the tree of life and from the holy city, which are written in this book,"* there was a transcendent awe that entered the place. An awe that seemed to say, "These words are, all by themselves, holy and enough."

We concluded that gathering in worship-filled, complete meltdown in the presence of God. Young adults today who were students then still come to me and tell me how that transcendent moment rocked their world and gave them a tender love for the Words.

I love the preamble of John's Gospel: *"In the beginning was the Word and the Word was with God, and the Word was God."* The Word wasn't *about* God; the Word *was* God. If I needed any further motivation to approach John's Book of Revelation with being sure about being in the Spirit when I approach it, that would certainly be it.

Sailing transcendent into a ravenous Holy Spirit Baptism, I long to be *known by the Word* and forever surrender the silly notion that, "I know my Bible."

Remember that sick wolf roaming around the edge of the flock? When the Book of Revelation is allowed to trumpet a revelation of Jesus Christ, that wolf will be left behind.

NASTY CAT IN THE BASEMENT

After 35 years of pastoral ministry I have found that there are very few *productive* options to hold to when it comes to the subject of the "endtimes." The following is a sampling to illustrate what I mean:

A. You can try to ignore it because it is too complicated.

B. Ignore it because, "It isn't my gifting to teach that sort of thing."

C. Ignore it because it is frankly too scary.

D. Ignore it because it is too controversial and it might split my church.

E. Go after it and sink into the multiple complications (and potentially sinking genuine discipleship).

F. Go after it and pretend it is my gift to teach it (while secretly using one of many books written by the specialists on the dates, timelines, and current geopolitical dynamics).

G. Go after it and scare the pants off most thinking people and ignore the terror in the eyes of children.

> H. Go after it and identify my church as one of the "Pre," "Post," "A," "Mid," blah, blah, blah categories.

As to A through D in the "Ignoring it" category, it is like greeting guests into your home and warning them that you have a nasty cat in the basement when and if you see them approaching the basement door.

"Whoa! Trust me. You don't want to go down there. We have this, a...pet...cat. The stench alone is bad, not to mention the rabies. Why do we keep it? Well, it was my grandmother's cat...she mysteriously died from rabies... but we promised to care for dear old Nasty. So please, stay here on the main floor."

As to E through H in the "going after it" category, it can be like keeping the cat on the main floor and dear old Nasty loves it when company comes to visit!

"Oh-oh—ha-ha-ha! There he goes again, claiming territory! Don't worry. Your shoes should smell better in a month or so. Say, by the way, do you have your rabies vaccinations up to date?"

I've chosen an entirely different path. I euthanized old Nasty several years ago. The basement was a beast to clean, but the whole house smells much better these days.

Occasionally, a guest shows up at my house with his own nasty cat. That's really annoying, but I've learned to keep a cat euthanizing kit right at my front door.

Through the years people have learned that they are always welcome in my home, but they better leave their nasty cat in their own basement terrorizing their own children. Apparently, some folks prefer living with a vicious, smelly, rabid cat over living the abundant life.

As for me, and my house? The Lion of the Tribe of Judah lives triumphantly in every room and His Kingdom is coming, day by day, *on earth, as it is in Heaven.* The smell is heavenly....

$10 Rambler Theology

When I was 16 my dad promised me he would buy my first car. The only caveat to this tantalizing teenage dream was that he would observe my driving behavior and purchase a car that he felt was equal to my level of maturity. Four months into my test, Dad drove up with a 1959 Rambler, which he found rotting in a backyard and bought for $10.

Painted with house paint, two of the four doors rusted completely into useless oblivion (the two useful doors were on the passenger side), this finely crafted piece of automotive genius was my dad's way of trying to tell me something.

When it rained, the house paint drooled off the fenders of this Rambler and onto the driveway. The chrome letters in the grill that once proudly spelled, "RAMBLER" were reduced to "-AM-LE-." Since my humility was not so much chosen as it was imposed upon me, I took the low road approach to my father's object lesson. I decided to run this "thing" into the ground. I drove it harder than any car should ever be driven.

I'll spare you the details, but suffice it to say that I was a geeky, yankee Duke of Hazard with a Private No Class "Amle" and not a General Lee. That dumb car had no better sense than to last a complete year! My dad had successfully taught me a valuable life lesson.

Let's take a few moments to strain this analogy for all it's worth.

I walked past a "Christian" section of a book sales rack the other day at a large retail outlet. On the cover of the most prominent book for sale in the name of Jesus, for all of shopping America to see, is a full color picture of a nuclear bomb. The author wants us all to know that God is fixated on His wristwatch, the Middle East is in the oven, and our "goose" is almost cooked. So I ask you, with the apparent popularity of this kind of tripe, is it possible that God, our heavenly Father, has allowed for a theology that matches our maturity level?

Is He standing back and allowing for us to be sufficiently humbled by this embarrassingly shallow interpretation of the treasury of the Scriptures? How many widely varying predictions of the *Late Great Planet Earth* have to be dead wrong before we look to the Holy Spirit for a more complete and soul-satisfying revelation of Jesus Christ?

In fact, one small comfort I hold with regard to this $10 rusted theo-mobile is that it is being driven into the ground. The only doom I predict is that "soon and very soon" its head will warp, the transmission will fall out, and this miserable heap will eventually have to be towed to history's junkyard.

If the devil cannot get us interested in outright miserable lifestyles, it seems no stretch to me that he would have us obsessed with self-destruction that is labeled "holy" so that we will not effectively exercise our faith for the healing of the nations. Why would I pray or believe for a nation to be healed if I am taught that that nation might be a pawn for God's "showdown at high noon"?

Here's another intriguing question for you: Why would I have any true vested interest to pray and act for the Kingdom of God to come on earth, just as it is in Heaven, if I am convinced that everything is just hooked up to God's timetable for a group of angry little nations who have been bitterly fighting each other for the past ka-zillion years?

What if God's timetable (if such a thing exists) is more rightly connected to the Body of Christ growing up and becoming a magnificent partner of and mirror image to Jesus Christ? What if the metaphors and the artistic, poetic majesty of books of the Bible like "The Revelation of Jesus Christ" held explosive spiritual secrets waiting for hungry, curious, insatiably and voraciously eager seekers to find a *True and Irresistible Spirituality*? What if some of us decided that we would rather walk to that goal than to drive a contribution to the spiritual pollution that has been killing the ozone of God's Highest and Best?

And, by the way, hasn't the greatest enemy of "best" always been "good"? Have we settled for some "good" teaching on the catastrophic judgment of God because it is far more entertaining and much less demanding of our faith for the healing of the nations? Wouldn't the "best" use of our vision and faith be that the nations would beat their swords into plowshares (see Mic. 4:3) due to a planet soaking of an outrageous flooding of the Holy Spirit on *all humanity* (see Joel 2:28)?

It seems to me that we have pulled up to far too many stranded people by the side of the road in our oil-burning junker, stuck our heads out the window and choked through the smoke, "Hey! Need a ride?" By now, we should have figured out why they keep turning down our offer. We thought we looked cool when in reality we really just looked dumb and too many people just don't want to be seen riding in our "-AM-LE-."

The Father has something else waiting for mature, responsible sons and daughters. He would like to pimp our ride….

Chapter 19

"Just a Good-Looking Guy..."

I'm just a good-looking guy
speaking on his behalf.
—Randy Dean

(Trust me, read the whole chapter.)

The Body of Christ has been profoundly influenced by some among us who are sleazy salesmen of a fatalistic dispensational eschatology. So prolific is their bottom line, these high profile few have too much to lose to recant their teachings; that is, assuming they were so inclined.

My blessing in life is that I have nothing to lose and no hill to climb and bleed for, other than Jesus Christ and Him crucified.

Please understand that it is not my intention here to battle their sales pitch, line upon dreadful line. In other places throughout this book I've used wit and spoof (Nasty Cat and $10 Rambler) to melt your defenses, if present. If not present, then I hope I've equipped you with good humor for conversations with others who do have their defenses prepared.

My aim here is to call the reader to look again and again and again into the Transcendent Supremacy of the Kingdom of God as beautifully adorned and expressed in the Life of Jesus Christ. If I can, in any measure, small or great, grant you permission to fully *"know Him"* (Phil. 3:10), I am convinced that any, and I mean any, teaching that intentionally or, as is the case most of time, unintentionally diminishes *Him* will slide off you like snow slides off a warming cabin roof.

Hang on tight with me through the following process. With every word you read here, ask the Holy Spirit to be the amazing tutor He loves to be, and I believe that by the end of this chapter you will be the possessor of majesty from Heaven. Not because I said it was so, but because the Holy Spirit will be faithful to speak words inside you that I don't even know how to type.

THE LIFE OF JESUS CHRIST

Jesus lived and walked the earth 2,000 years ago and He said, *"He who has seen Me has seen the Father"* (John 14:9). For years I smugly acted like I completely understood the words and the chapter I just quoted. But actually seeing Him and knowing that I am seeing the Father has taken me further than I once dreamed possible.

Leading up to the quote (verse 6) above we find this: *"Jesus said to him* [Thomas], *'I am the way, and the truth, and the life; no one comes to the Father but through Me.'"* A narrow-see (remember, rhymes with *Pharisee*) vision looks right past the potential treasure of these words and sees, "If you don't come to God the Father through Jesus you're going to hell." Or, "If you come to the Father in the name of Jesus you will go to Heaven."

I believe that Jesus was painting a far more glorious spirit portrait than either of those conclusions.

You could say verse 6 this way, "Jesus said, 'I am the means of a journey (the way). I am the unveiling (the truth). I am the Reality of living (the life). No one arrives at, gets near to, or even has the foggiest notion of who the Father is, but through Me. Through Me as in, side to side, first to last, end to end, day by growing day, *transcending all other contemplations and going all the way through Me."*

And, if you absolutely need a pinch of evangelical garnish, here you go: "Any other way imposes hellish limitations that will trap you right where you are. The law and the prophets will make perfect sense to your natural mind. But going this way will take you into the deep end of Heaven's pool. And where you are, is where you are going."

All of this is vital to get you to the conclusion I promised earlier…soak it in a moment. Ready?

The Life of Jesus Christ—The Present

Now as it pertains to God the Father, every theory, every thought, every proposition, every concept, every premise, every feeling about the world, every view of the "end of the world" must pass through Jesus. Even every Word of the Old and New Testaments must pass through Jesus.

He is The Word and The Word was God, long before there was the leather-bound treasure we hold in our hands. No translation matches the accuracy of Him.

If I impose a view of God the Father that does not go through Jesus as in, side to side, first to last, end to end, day by growing day, transcending all other contemplations and going all the way through Jesus, it becomes a faulty view of God at best and deception at worst.

Here's an easy illustration: "Hey, Jesus! We caught this city in the act of adultery, fornication, and all around general nastiness! The law says that the soul that sins shall surely die! We think a hurricane would be in order to punish this city. What do *You* say?"

I hope the answer is obvious. If it isn't, read John 8:1-11… quickly! Now, let's climb up another rung on the ladder.

Remember this as well. Jesus said in Matthew 5:17 that He didn't come to do away with the Law and the Prophets but to fulfill them. The word used for *fulfill* here has fascinating implications. It means "to make replete, to cram a net, level up a hollow, to satisfy, execute, finish, accomplish, and to complete."

So now, if I want to come to the Father about any word of prophetic doom, I have to go *through* Jesus. If I find a prophetic picture in the Bible that looks an awful lot like a boiling storm, I have to roll that baby up, put it under my arm, and take it and me right *through* Jesus.

Everywhere we go today, it seems we are passing through metal detectors. Airports, shopping malls, schools, sporting events, grocery stores, and yes, even churches. I love these things. As soon as I see where I am going with any crowd of people and I know the metal detector is on task, I feel relatively sure that most of the guns on the other side of that thing belong to the good guys.

I know they aren't foolproof, but please don't tell me how many bad guys can get through a metal detector with a gun, because, at least on things like this, ignorance is bliss. Besides, I don't want you to mess with my illustration here.

Imagine, if you will, that a security company somewhere announces the world's first perfect metal detector. Their claim is, "If you have so much as looked at a gun in the last 24 hours, our detector will know it." Do you think that they'd have a pretty good chance of selling such a product if after a reasonable testing run they proved their claim? I do, and I also think that any venue that would use their product would likely advertise that said detector was on the job at this event or establishment.

In my early training for ministry and the years that followed I was taught to believe and I dutifully adhered to a basic premise for the endtimes that is thematic to whatever version or variance is being served. Here it is:

…there is one last blast of God's wrath coming.

However else you cook it down, whatever else is felt to be necessary for the 144,000 and whatever group they really belong to, how 666 might be a computer chip or a tattoo, if it's seven years or 3.5 years, whether it's seven churches or seven church ages—one thing is absolutely needed: God's wrath. For most dispensational endtime aficionados, if not all, it is this one matter that really *matters*…

…there is one last blast of God's wrath coming.

In some circles it gets some decoration to make it more appealing for conspiracy theorists (don't get me started). In other circles it is fine-tuned to natural disasters. Most groups have the redemption of national Israel parked in the middle of their purpose. One particularly nasty group has ethnic Israel as God's target for wrath. But it is definitely still about one thing…

…there is one last blast of God's wrath coming.

This is why some of these persuasions *need* the rapture…to spare Christians the terrible reality that… (see my P.S. at the end of this chapter)…

…there is one last blast of God's wrath coming.

Make no mistake about it. Everyone has Scriptures completely lined up for an ironclad, debate-winning, shut up and sit down, "there it is in chapter and verse" proof. One small problem:

Jesus.

With every theory, proof-text, newspaper heading, and the latest numerology formula proving once and for all that the politician we hate most is assuredly the anti-christ…there stands Jesus…waiting for us to go *through* Him with all of that in our carry-on luggage.

This is one of those times in the book that I am tempted to include a very long Scripture quotation, but I will remain true to my challenge in the Introduction.

Read Isaiah 53. It is a panoramic prophetic vision of the crucifixion. Read it with the Holy Spirit singing the verses in your heart, and read it slowly so you can truly learn the melody and the cadence of every certainty the prophet saw.

Slow down at verse 11…listen carefully. The Holy Spirit wants to sing for you the way He sang for the prophet: *"As a result of the anguish of His soul, He will see it and be satisfied; By His knowledge the Righteous One, My servant, will justify the many, as He will bear their iniquities."*

Did you hear it? Did you see it? Do you feel it? God is satisfied.

In absorbing the full blunt force of humanity's failure, His Son was despised, forsaken, a man of sorrows, acquainted with grief, shunned and utterly shamed. *Smitten and afflicted of God. Pierced through, crushed, scourged, oppressed and slaughtered! AND GOD IS SATISFIED!*

I believe that the horror Isaiah saw and reported in these verses is the collective of all other horrors of the fall of humankind and the potential of any wrath required as justice. The last and lasting blast of God's wrath, however you choose to define wrath—it is finished.

God is satisfied.

No flood, firestorm, war, hurricane, earthquake, or misery of any description is God's instrument of venting any measure of His need for being satisfied! Flood and misery may come and go, but our insight to all of it need simply be for compassion for the victims!

No wonder Paul suggests in First Corinthians 2:1-5 that he would walk into a gathering and take a reading—is there a revelation of Christ crucified in this bunch? Is Jesus Christ crucified their final satisfaction for all wrath and judgment? Or does their God need anger management courses? Is their God as satisfied as Isaiah 53:11 predicted He would be when He looked on His Son's anguish in order to justify the many? Are these people freed by the crucified Christ from any further "need" for wrath on anybody, including them!

Because if they are, there will be a demonstration of the Spirit and of power and their faith will be in the power of God and not the wisdom of people. This is a place and a people where the Kingdom of God has an opportunity to be fully demonstrated. Its Transcendence will leave people in a wonder-filled state of shouting, "Look what God is doing!"

Remember the layer of truth we laid in the opening of this chapter. We cannot journey into any significant portion of the Father's nature until and unless we pass through Jesus. Go through Him and God's character becomes an open book. Step around Him and hundreds of passages in the Bible look like mysterious spooky eyes leering at you from a dark forest on a scary howling autumn night.

As surely as the ubiquitous metal detector will find that gun in your pocket, so Jesus' final sacrifice will detect any and all leftover need in our hearts for that one last blast of God's wrath on earth.

I have sat through more than a few prophecy meetings with that uneasy feeling in the pit of my stomach that something was wrong. Scriptures were racing up and down the concourses but I routinely found myself wishing for that transcendent metal detector. It sure looked like too many weapons (one is enough!) had made their way to the gate and I simply let those flights of fancy leave the airport without me.

Like some of you, I've watched a few too many Christian television commentators doing their best to look and sound like Walter Cronkite (if you're under 50, Google it). Pictures of wars and rumors of wars, and nations rising up against nations scroll through the background pictures while they recite Scriptures so fast I'm left with no other conclusion but to say, "Wow!" (This is part of my purpose in asking you to go to your very own Bible and search for every reference I am giving you. See the words with your own eyes and view the entire landscape surrounding a passage.)

But "wow" isn't in my vocabulary when I take calls from people new to my flock, or the outsiders who trust me, or the very young or, in some cases, older folks whose nearest companion is the television. In many cases these are people who are innocently channel surfing, hear a Bible verse and decide to stop awhile and be edified.

"Holy cow, pastor! I was watching this Christian show last night and I heard that the Y2K of the 666 with the 144,000 living in 7 years of Babylonian Nostradamus prophetic nuclear Middle East timetable of the harlot riding the beast's European 10 chariots through the valley of Armageddon while the United States continues to have no better sense than to say, 'peace, peace' when the reality is the two witnesses get killed and sudden destruction is coming sometime in December something, something in the year 2012…maybe…but if not then, by 2020 because there are 20 reasons why it's all over by then…and this is all in the Bible…. Is that true, pastor?"

Someone once said that being absurd is the best way to illustrate absurdity. That's all I've got to say about that (a

Forrest Gump voice in your head is required for that comment to work).

GOT TELEOLOGY?

Truth is, we've all got some kind of teleology. It's a matter of what kind it is that needs a thorough sorting out.

It could be said that teleology is the study of what we see out in front of us and how it directs our lives today. More technically it is a school of thought that says all things are designed for or directed toward a final result and that there is an inherent purpose in everything, which then feeds into that result.

WHAT YOU SEE IS WHAT YOU'LL BE

If I saturate my vision with signs of cataclysm that confirm my belief that the world must grow more miserable leading to the return of Christ, I will arrange my life around the misery and call it "faith."

Someone said to me once that they were pleased Jimmy Carter had been elected because, "things will get bad enough now to set the stage for the return of Christ."

When I was ten I went to a Vacation Bible School with a family in southern Illinois. One morning the teacher of our boy's class leaned over the table and told the three or four of us there, "You boys won't see your 14th birthday...

not on this earth anyway." I didn't sleep that night. My teleology took a nasty hit.

I am pleased to announce that I saw my 14th birthday on this earth and 40 more since. It would also be a pleasure to tell you that I never took another one of those nasty hits to my teleology, but I can't.

In the mid-1970s during my Bible college experience, a professor turned on the radio so our class on Homiletics (how to preach...I'm still learning) could listen to the latest news from the Middle East. I honestly can't tell you which war or invasion it was. When the broadcast was done the teacher turned off the radio and announced that he was certain we wouldn't need the education we were there to get. I didn't sleep that night either.

In November of the year our first child Libby was born, on the very day Ginger and I brought her home, someone mused, "I'm happy for you, but it is such a terrible time for a child to be born into. Things are so bad, any day now I'm sure we will be leaving this old weary world." All three of us didn't sleep that night...Libby had her own reasons.

Then, it was 1988 and there were "88 Reasons" the rapture would certainly happen that year...and yet another little Christian book was terrorizing the countryside.

Somewhere in the milieu of sleepless nights and dumb comments I decided to find out what my own teleology was. I didn't know it was teleology then, but I sure knew what the destructive effects could be if it was rooted in fear and faithlessness. I had heard one too many songs celebrating how tired we all were of this soon to be incinerated planet!

These were the early days of my discovery of the message of the Kingdom of God. Just the mention of those three words made my spine straighten. It called to something in the deep of me and I knew it was something in the deep of God.

I am happy to report that today there's no healing for my hope. I am hopelessly hopeful, incurably whole, and beyond help for the view I hold of the God I love and the world He loves. I'm positively giddy about the future and drunk with a Holy Spirit induced high that won't let me go!

Today my good cheer will not let me go where the bell ringers ding-donging doomsday love to go. God has given me a theology with a teleology that has a methodology of an ontology rooted in the very nature of God as revealed in His Christology. It *Is* that simple.

If you need any help on those terms, take a moment and feel free to do some research…we've got plenty of time.

Research and time—those are commodities that some sleazy salesmen of end-times products won't encourage you to use.

Martin Luther King Jr. once said, "I believe that unarmed truth and unconditional love will have the final word in reality." Look at each one of those delicious words.

This quote is one of the many points of teleology that produced Dr. King's Dream.

In a speech following his acceptance of the Nobel Prize for literature in 1950, William Faulkner said, "I decline to accept the end of man…. I believe that man will not only endure: he will prevail…because he has a soul, a spirit capable of compassion and sacrifice and endurance." He said this in the early days of the Cold War with the memory of pictures of two mushroom clouds fresh in the minds of most people on the planet. Humankind had just discovered the power to self-destruct.

But he resisted the teleology of failure by shouting back at it, "I decline to accept the end of man…."

There are voices in the Church today who, with unchained reach and unfettered volume, are declaring the opposite. To them, there is a violent "end" of human life based solely on the evil nature of humans. Nuclear holocaust like hailstones from God will be served up with a side dish of divinely inspired 15.0 earthquakes…and those are just the appetizers! Their teleology *welcomes* the thief, whose goals are killing, stealing, and destroying.

These voices will always conclude their foray to the edge of an apocalyptic cliff and attempt to redeem their claim to have good news by cheerfully reminding us, "When you see all these things, our redemption draweth nigh! The King is coming!"

Here's what I have to say to that: The King came! The King reigns now! Our redemption isn't "nigh"—it is finished! Only when we saturate ourselves in the Transcendent Supremacy of the First Coming will we have any capacity for comprehension of the Second Coming!

"But, pastor! Haven't you read the Book of Revelations?" No, I have not; but I have read the Revelation of Jesus Christ, if that's what you are talking about. And, my, my, my, the optimism I live just rides ever higher. That part, where God says to John, "Come up here and I will show you what must take place after these things" just makes me squeal with delight, like a kid in a school yard recess "free for all" snowball fight.

When John gets yanked out of his earthbound funk by the power of the Holy Spirit, he sees a rainbow-laced throne, glimmering with jewel-like magnificence. That report alone makes *me* sound like a pessimist.

What I'm trying to say is that in the face of the very real dangers of the world in which we live, the Church cannot afford an anemic teleology that plays into the plans of the enemy of God's creation! If you believe "it all blows up" in the end, then, whether you know it or not, you welcome and possibly subconsciously enjoy every destructive incident that confirms your ultimate and final view of what you think to be God's purposes.

Unfortunately, if even at a subterranean level we are surrendered to any notion that the world cannot change, then for us, it will not change. Too many have Christianized the notion that the world cannot change and, indeed, must grow worse and worse, darker and darker. This has created an irresponsible theology, which subtly unplugs us from a vital faith for the healing of the nations.

The greater the nuclear arsenal of the world, the greater should be the arising of our faith for swords being converted into plowshares (see Mic. 4:3). Is this possible only at the Second Coming of Christ? I say it is possible because of the *First Coming of Christ....*

CHRIST CRUCIFIED IS ENOUGH!

Ephesians 1:10 says everything in Heaven and earth will be summed up in Christ. Therefore, my teleology is producing a sky-high faith for *everyday events* that will lead to that summation! ***Christ crucified and raised from the dead is enough!***

Now, before I close this chapter, let's go back to William Faulkner's quote and speech. It's loaded with a healthy teleology. (Google the whole speech with the quote, "I decline to accept the end of man.") His warning over 60 years ago was that if authors of *any kind* of literature stood among and watched the end of man, they would write not of the heart, *but of the glands.* They would write not of love, but of lust, of defeats in which nobody loses anything of value, of victories without hope and, worst of all, without pity or compassion.

In my view, even Christian literature slides into this morass and has unwittingly contributed to the pessimistic immoral culture we so despise! It seems to me that Faulkner has it right when he says that to believe in a catastrophic end is to surrender to the lowest common denominator of the human condition.

I believe the glory of the Scriptures paint something far deeper, more mystically profound than the surface view that makes God's book look like a collection of special effects for our movie entertainment.

So, tell me…Got Teleology? Is it brimming with unarmed truth and unconditional love? In your teleology, is Christ raised from the dead and victorious over the grave? Or is His resurrection just an anecdotal historical event for your personal future pleasure safely distant from this blue planet turned to ashes from God's fury?

In a Kingdom-based teleology the resurrection is an ongoing event. Ephesians 1 and 2 gloriously chronicle that, in order for us to even know what our true calling is, we each need a transcending enlightenment! The very same supremacy that blew the door off Jesus' tomb has blasted us upward into Heaven (while we live on earth).

What wonders await us are limited only by our desire.

I remember teaching these principles in some of the early days of my eyes being opened to real hope. A high school aged young lady came to me after the service and said, "Thank you for freeing me from the shame I have felt my whole life for just wanting to have a happy marriage and be a mom. I was told once that we cannot 'love this world' so much that we aren't ready at any minute to leave it. I could never reconcile my desires with that fear and I simply felt ashamed."

What wonders await us are limited only by our desire.

How's your teleology now?

PRACTICE, PRACTICE, PRACTICE...

Is it possible that there is nothing in God's way for the fulfillment of all His promises? Is it possible that the only thing left is for the Church to complete its task, equal to Jesus, as a final witness of the utter failure of satan's rebellion? (See Ephesians 3:10-11.) Is it possible that when Jesus said, on the cross, "It is finished," that He meant that very thing in the broadest possible terms?

Is it possible for God's final satisfaction to be ours? Because if it is, there is an amazing adventure of Kingdom Radiance waiting for us to explore.

Bill Johnson says, in *When Heaven Invades Earth*,

Many, if not most theologians, make the mistake of taking all the good stuff contained in the prophets and sweeping in under that mysterious rug called the Millennium....our propensity (is) to put off those things that require courage, faith, and action to another period of time. The mistaken idea is this: if it is good, it can't be for now.[1]

I would add this: if it is good, then it must be Jesus. If it isn't good, then it needs to go *through* Jesus.

With all that being said, the best way to conclude this chapter is to go back to John 14, starting at verse 12: *"Truly, truly I say to you, he who believes in Me, the works that I do shall he do also; and greater works than these shall he do; because I go to the Father. And whatever you ask in My name, that will I do, that the Father may be glorified in the Son. If you ask Me anything in My name, I will do it."*

That's amazing! Ask anything? Do greater works than Jesus? I guess He really did mean it on the cross when He said, "It is finished." There really isn't anything left to do but to glorify the Father with greater works than the Son.

The old world order died on the cross and a new world order is waiting for the Transcendent Supremacy of the Kingdom of God, which is at *our hands.*

Revelation 22:2 states that the leaves of the tree of life are for the healing of the nations. If healing nations is on our menu, I would suggest we routinely practice healing everywhere we go. Seeing a broken ankle healed is perfect practice for healing vertigo. Healing vertigo is perfect practice for healing cancer. Healing cancer is perfect practice for healing learning disabilities in children. Healing learning disabilities in children is perfect practice for healing families of the demonic effects of drug and alcohol abuse. Healing families of the demonic effects of drug and alcohol abuse is perfect practice for healing America. If medicine is a practice, shouldn't we learn from this natural order? One discovery leads to another and before you know it, a disease is conquered!

(Everything you just read is happening in the rural church I pastor. I love to tell people, "I pastor a church of 200 in a town of 15. We've reached our city for Jesus and now we're coming after yours!")

If you can't heal a nation today, why not practice on the next sinus infection that comes your way? When once and for all we are faithful with the little, He will make us rulers over much.

When the Lord obliterates our captivity to fables, we become like those who dream….

Hey! That gives me an idea…I'm going to start a new kind of Christian news broadcast, prepared for the fun that is coming!

"Good Evening, He's your Anchor, Jesus Christ, and I'm just a good-looking guy speaking on His behalf. My hair is amazing.

"At the top of our broadcast tonight a report just came in from Milwaukee, Wisconsin. A spokesperson for the county hospital has told us by phone that one of their janitors came to work this morning after going to what he called, 'An off-the-hook revival service' at a nearby church. He told this spokesperson, 'Jesus told me to go to work this morning and radiate *Him* while I mopped floors.' We are still at this hour trying to follow up on all the reports, but a visitor to the hospital told us, 'The whole place just started shaking! Suddenly, patients were walking out of their rooms asking what was going on. Physicians were frantically trying to attend to the commotion, when suddenly the building just filled with light! I personally had a cold, and it is gone! One nurse told me that several terminal patients have checked out and one lady who had been in a coma for a month came to the front desk asking for her clothes. I hear they just had to throw a blanket around her!' As to the janitor, when he was last seen he was dancing with his mop on the top floor."

Wow!

P.S. For anyone reading this, friend or foe, who absolutely needs a rapture because First Thessalonians 4:17 says we will be "caught up," you are certainly welcome to it. Just do yourself and me four simple favors:

1. Unplug your need for a rapture from any view you have of that "one last blast of wrath from God" on the bad people.

2. Unplug your need for a rapture from any and all timetables. I'm begging you here. Use all your laminated charts for place mats.

3. Uproot yourself from anything that even remotely resembles an escapist mentality. Fly

away, if you must, but don't allow one scintilla of thought about "this old wicked world" or "lately I've got leaving on my mind" or any number of the pitiful escapist variables that exist.

4. And don't expect me to sing about it with you. The only rapture (as in ecstasy, delight, and bliss) I will sing about is the Transcendent Supremacy of the Kingdom of God and the radiance that beams in me as a result of its life-transforming power to *stay on earth and overcome.*

Thank you. Have a nice flight.

ENDNOTE

1. Bill Johnson, *When Heaven Invades Earth* (Destiny Image Publishers, 2005), 34.

Chapter 20

MO OR JO?

Maybe God will change His mind
when you change yours.
—Randy Dean

Two men in the Old Testament had amazing and parallel callings from God. Their stories serve as a contrast in leadership style and heart that we would do well to soak into our conscience.

Moses and Jonah are these two men. Both had a relationship with God that bear little or no resemblance to anyone I know and yet their strengths and weaknesses look an awful lot like many I know, myself included.

First, to Moses. When Israel decided that Moses was gone too long on his mountain retreat, they invented a new religion and made a golden calf. God slipped this information into the morning devotional with Moses and said, *"Let Me alone, that My anger may burn against them, and that I may destroy them; and I will make of you a great nation."* Did you catch that?

First of all, God said to a man, *"Let Me alone..."* or "Get out of the way..."! Do you know that sometimes God will give you a command for the purpose of shining a great big light on your heart? I remind people of that very fact when they run up to me and announce, "God told me to do this thing...what do you think?"

I think you need to take a very serious inventory of your motives. I think that God may be after something far less obvious than what your immediate impression might be. I also think that if you can't see what's happening here, then nothing I say will change that.

Second, in a naked appeal to this man's pride, God offered to make *"a great nation"* out of Moses. Thousands of church splits have been born out of this very scenario. I don't doubt that God has spoken to some people about how He could do great things with them if only they would blow off the group they are with and go start a new group. The problem is that this kind of person may also be missing the greater Transcendence of God healing them of their dysfunctional ego.

On the first account, Moses did *not* get out of the way so that God could smoke Israel, and on the second account Moses made an equally naked appeal back to the character of God and said, *"Turn from Your burning anger and change Your* [almighty] *mind!"* (I added "almighty" just for grins.) In fact, Moses later added that if God was going to fry Israel, then He should start by lighting up Moses (see Exod. 32).

Too many current religious leaders would have stepped aside with a smug smile and given God their blessing, found the nearest public platform or television camera, and announced, "God told me…." To say nothing of the fact that they would have gleefully accepted the honor of becoming the founder of a new great nation/ministry.

There's another Old Testament story that comes to mind here as well. God told Jonah to give the city of Nineveh a 40-day notice that a terrorist act would blow them up…or something akin to that. Did Jonah do his best Moses imitation? Nope.

He looked more like too many of us. He ran right into the digestive tract of a fish in order to hide from his God-given responsibility. When it finally occurred to him that being obedient might be better than becoming fish manure, he repented and the fish puked him up within a three-day walk of Nineveh. Upon his arrival, he preached, Nineveh did some serious repenting, and the terrorist plot was canceled. End of the story? Nope.

Jonah pouted and prayed to die. In the midst of his praying to die, he admitted that he knew the character of God so well that he said, *"I fled…for I knew that You are a gracious and compassionate God, slow to anger and abundant in lovingkindness, and One who relents concerning calamity* [terrorist attacks]."

In other words, he wanted them to get what they deserved so that the end result of destruction would make him look like a real prophet. For some, there is nothing so satisfying as seeing a disaster that looks like you predicted it. *This kind of person would rather see dramatic problems than to see dramatic solutions!*

I have had the painful occasion to come across a few modern Jonahs. I remember one Rev. Dr. Jonah who related how that just prior to Katrina, he saw a vision while visiting New Orleans. In his vision he saw that the entire city would soon be under water. He felt that he had no choice but to get that word out to as many people in the Big Easy as he could.

Here's what would have really impressed me: armed with this revelation, if he had moved to New Orleans to fast and pray. Then, if he'd followed that by standing on the shores of the Gulf to successfully stop Katrina with the Word of the Kingdom. *And then*, if he'd turned to the city and said, "Our God is a gracious and compassionate God, slow to anger and abundant in lovingkindness, and One who relents concerning calamity. Come to Him today!" (Maybe Katrina's devastation was not so much the bungling of FEMA and President Bush…maybe the bungling was this prophet. Just a thought.)

It seems to me that God is looking for something deeper in those of us who represent Him than just the ability to scare the pants off the nearest bystander with predictions of disaster or pronouncements of God's "will." I know there is much more that needs to be said about all of the above, however, for the sake of this chapter, let it be summed up that more of us need to look like Moses and less of us like Jonah!

What if your one life means the difference in historic change or historic calamity? Would you choose to pay the price to introduce change or would you take the path of least resistance and step aside and watch calamity with the explanation, "Yes, it must have been God's will and I predicted it too"?

Once, as a young pastor, I found myself totally frustrated...once...OK, twice. Anyway, after one particularly frustrating Sunday morning I shook a few hands and made my way to my hiding place...a tiny one-hole bathroom.

I looked in the mirror at my drained face and said, "I can't do this anymore, God. I'm through with this bunch." To my surprise and pleasure I heard Him say, "Good. If next Sunday you get the same lack of response, then I am through with them too."

The following Sunday couldn't come fast enough for me. I gave my message preparation my very best, just to be sure. Sunday came, I rained a beauty of a message down on those folks, and sure enough...nothing. It felt like I had thrown seeds on a concrete floor.

I shook a few hands and made my way back to my one-hole bathroom hiding place. The face in the mirror was the same forlorn guy I had seen a week prior. I said, "Well, God! That's it! You said You were done with them and I am too!"

The answer came back fast and stark. He said, "You wouldn't make much of a Moses, would you?"

That moment was one of the most profound wake-up calls I have ever experienced. I stayed in that church for several years and prayed every day for God to change my heart and spare His people.

He did both.

The next time you think that God has given you a word about how evil somebody is or how deserving of judgment some group or nation seems, I dare you to stand up to God, remind Him of what His Son has done on the cross, and see if you're still alive when the encounter is done. The scare alone will do you some good.

And maybe God will change His mind (see Exod. 32:14) when you change yours!

P.S. Predicting a California earthquake is about as impressive as predicting a winter snowstorm here in Wisconsin. Frost and fault lines have nothing to do with God being angry. Get over it.

That's your free part…you may proceed.

Chapter 21

A Culture of Life

Mugger with a gun to Jack Benny, notorious cheapskate: "Your money or your life.... Well...what are you waiting for?" Jack Benny: "I'm thinking, I'm thinking!"

The death of Jesus Christ was brutal and vulgar. It demonstrated the worst of human systems gone mad. God allowed all of our most confused, bureaucratic, religious stupidity a full and tortured expression on the Body of Jesus. Every human system participated and satan kicked back at the end of the day, looked up at Heaven and asked, "Hey, God! What do You think of Your creation now? Still think it's 'good'?"

God answered three days later. With the physical resurrection of Jesus God has forever stated, "What I have made *is good*. Creation was kissed in the beginning and now it has been twice kissed."

Some elements of Christianity are totally obsessed with total depravity and original sin. They are fond of announcing that we are born in sin. The follow up to that is the mantra, "We are just sinners saved by grace."

Here's an honest question I have about that: how would a mentally healthy person respond to someone less mentally healthy who repeatedly referred to his children in that manner? "Yep, these kids are depraved. Like, totally. It's a good thing for them they're born under my roof. I'm a big enough guy to just let it go…otherwise I'd have to kill 'em."

Let's take that a step further. What if that same mentally unhealthy person was trying to adopt another child and they used you as a reference for the adoption agency? Would your reference be less than a ringing endorsement? Is it possible that this same scenario is undermining our endorsement of Father God to a world of spiritual children dying for adoption?

So, what about *now*—post resurrection and post ascension? Aren't we thoroughly and transcendently born *again?* This time, born again *right* and righteous?" At what point do we start being the New Creation?

I love the message of the cross because it leaves us with a satisfied God. But, make no mistake about it, the cross is not God's final statement. *Life* is God's final statement! And since it is, the implications are off the charts for what we have been called to be and to do.

Jesus said, "The thief has come to steal, kill, and destroy. I have come that you might have life and that with flourish, dynamic and complete animation!" The Church is called to be a culture of Life. Not a parenthesis holding cell, awaiting life after death.

We are a culture of Life filled with belly laughs, loud glorious singing, expansive divine curiosity, entrepreneurial inventiveness, and a passionate exploration of the Life and Character of God that might challenge safe theological boxes. The vacated grave of Jesus is the genius of God, which calls every hungry heart to reject death in all of its expressions.

In John 10:10 we are told that Jesus came so that we could have abundant life. The word *abundant* there means superabundant, superior, excessive, and BEYOND! It is animated, dynamic, transcendent, insuperable, and preeminent! Somebody somewhere is going to leap into this culture of Life and live it for all it's worth…some day.

This is my destiny. Will you join me?

Chapter 22

HAIL, MARY!

I love Mary, the mother of Jesus. Her story, her life, her spirit makes me want to shout out, "Hail, Mary!"

I heard a great man of God, David du Plessis, say, "Catholics worship her, which is a mistake, but Protestants ignore her, which is an *equal* mistake." In other words, to make her a god is to miss the power of the reality that God wants to be wonderfully glorified in little, simple, normal human beings. But, to minimize her because some rigid religionist might accuse us of being too "catholic-y" (an accusation I have actually heard) is just as evil as making her the fourth member of the Godhead. The Gospel of Luke says that her faith made her sing, *"All generations will call me blessed and declare me happy and to be envied!"* (Luke 1:48 AMP).

Pretty heady stuff for a peasant girl living under the political boot of Roman bloodthirstiness. Not to mention the sheer spiritual audacity of her faith in the atmosphere of a stale and dead Jewish religion. The fact that the angel

Gabriel came to her in a full material appearance should say more to us than we usually accredit to this kind of event. Angels don't appear with good news to folks who are not inclined to believe such an outrageous event. She was clearly a firebrand of faith prior to her visitation. Pretty heady stuff indeed!

Now, what about you and me? Are we inclined to believe that God is looking for more peasants to exalt in the face of political and material arrogance? Do we have *any* expectations of angelic visitations? Is there *anyone* out there walking in *any* kind of faith that is rocking *any* ships of state or status quo? How about some virgin spiritual soil ready for a Kingdom Word that will give birth to some Transcendent Supremacy on the earth *as it is* in Heaven?

Think of it like this: If we believed about ourselves what Catholicism believes about Mary, we would all be better off!

We simply must stop reading the Bible like we're visiting a museum. It's a calling! It's a dare! It's a document 1,400 years in the making, of prophets, poets, and warriors, relating how God is fishing for people who are willing to risk everything for an evening stroll on stormy waters.

Praying, "Thy Kingdom come, Thy will be done, on earth *as it is* in heaven…" is pure stupidity if we are not ready, eager, and willing to make room for Gabriel to challenge our normal sensibilities about what can or cannot logically (not to mention *bio*-logically) happen!

Heck, I'd settle for a chat with an angel named Fritz if it meant being chosen for making Kingdom history!

Where are the Marys of the 21st century? If it's you, let me be the first to shout out a "Hail" in your direction. Hail, Fred! Hail, Jane! C'mon, let's pray for and then live some Kingdom disruption on earth *as it is* in Heaven.

REMEMBER THE USSR?

In 1982 I invited a handful of young people to our church to share their stories of smuggling Bibles into the old Soviet Union. I remember sitting on the front pew weeping as I listened to their stories and soaked in the beauty of the slides they were showing.

When a picture of them walking in Red Square came up on the screen, I prayed, "God, I want to walk those bricks and pray, 'Thy Kingdom come, Thy will be done, on earth as it is in Heaven.'"

In 1989 my wife and I got that opportunity. Through a series of events too long to repeat here, we were invited to be part of a small team whose purpose was twofold: smuggle Bibles and help two young men from Leningrad get their student visas to come to the states for ministry training. I had a tiny personal agenda of my own…to walk the bricks of Red Square praying for the Kingdom of God to come, right there.

The whole trip was an adventure of a lifetime. When you look someone in the eye who has prayed his entire life for a Bible and you hand him that answer to prayer, you will never forget the transcendence of that exchange. I'm in that transcendent moment again as I write these words.

We have a treasure chest full of experiences from that trip. Witnessing, praying for the sick, encouraging the underground church and securing those student visas I mentioned earlier. One of those students, Dmitri Polikov, is today a pastor in St. Petersburg (formerly Leningrad), overseeing 500 churches. (When we met him all he had was a handwritten New Testament, which he had personally translated with nothing but a paperback dictionary to work from.)

All other events of the trip aside, I was like bacon on a frying pan waiting to get to Red Square. When our taxi drove to the edge of that national secular holy ground, I launched out of the door. As soon as my toes touched the bricks, that prayer was rumbling in my spirit and out of my mouth.

I was in Heaven! Literally! I stomped around gleefully, from Lenin's Tomb to the Kremlin Wall. I vibrated the Transcendent Domain of a Kingdom of Absolute Supreme Infallibility.

Imagine my delight when not many months later the world was hearing the news that the USSR was crumbling! Communism was being washed out of power by a populace starved for freedom.

Am I so naïve as to believe that I did that? *No!* What I *do* believe is that I was one more "bean" falling on a scale in the heavenlies. I do not know how many thousands of believers preceded me in this childlike exercise. I do not know how many Russian believers may have died a martyr's death for the sake of that prayer. While we were there we did meet a handful of brothers and sisters in Moscow, for instance, who had suffered unthinkably for simple acts of faith.

Here's my point: every one of us is a potential, invisible, unknown Mary. One moment of one act of faith in the face of a complete impossibility is what we are asked to do, every day and in every footstep we take. The point is *none* of us knows which one of those "beans" will fall on a heavenly scale and become the tipping point.

I recommend Malcolm Gladwell's book, *The Tipping Point,* for all the research on the "beans." What captures my imagination is a simple summation printed on the jacket of the book. To me this quote alone is worth the price of the entire book. "Just as a single person can start an epidemic of the flu, so too can a small but precisely targeted push cause a fashion trend, the popularity of a new product, or a drop in the crime rate."[1]

Mary's little-ness is her greatness. The Transcendent Supremacy of the Kingdom only needed one seed to drop (see Matt. 13:31).

If the mighty intellectual, the apostle Paul, was humble enough to recognize the Transcendent Supremacy in sending out handkerchiefs *"carried from his body to the sick"* (Acts 19:11-12), then we should certainly believe and practice on a daily basis the transference of transcendence; from bricks in Red Square to shopping carts in parking lots!

I am widely known for my shopping cart ministry. It used to be that I would drive into a parking lot of any variety of retail stores and find myself boiling over the lazy habit of people leaving their shopping carts in parking spaces that could otherwise be used for the novel idea of parking a car.

At first, I considered myself heroic because I would park my car in one of the few available spaces that wasn't occupied by a shopping cart, angrily grab a stray cart and put it where someone else should have put it, in the shopping cart corral. I was the king of smug servanthood.

One day while crashing yet another stray into the OK Corral, God spoke to me. It was actually more in the form of a public service announcement: "Is anger over little matters eating your spiritual energy? Are you cursing more and blessing less? Are you doing a good thing in a bad way? What kind of deposit are you leaving in your wake? There is a better way. The next time you see a stray shopping cart, I want you to bless it and everyone who touches it. Open yourself to My Spirit, listen to My Voice, and send these carts into the possibilities of My Kingdom."

Shortly after this rebuke, I was pushing a shopping cart beyond the corral and all the way into the store. The Holy Spirit had me riveted to pictures of families who would be coming to this store, pushing this very cart and in need of a wide variety of miracles. I saw an angry dad scolding and shaming little children while a codependent mom straggled behind. I saw a single mom wrestling to carry a baby on her hip and manage toddlers in tow through a busy parking lot. I heard the Holy Spirit call out "cancer, diabetes, high blood pressure, and much more."

When I entered the store I was weeping, but I was blessing that cart with Kingdom Come possibilities! All at once, I came to my senses, looked down at the handle and saw a message from Heaven literally printed between my hands!

It said, "Thank You."

I am painfully aware that all this sounds terribly naïve on my part. It might even sound as bad as a pregnant teenage girl claiming that the Holy Spirit did this to her. I'll take that risk. Kingdom miracles are at your hand. Dismiss them if you will or live looking for Kingdom Come moments. Who knows which moment will tip the scale?

And by the way, I didn't even need a shopping cart in the visit to the store I just described. I realized that somewhere in aisle 4.

Bond-slave of the Impossible

Mary embodies every quality which ought to typify all of Christianity. And just for the sake of clarity let me say again that while Catholicism worships her as a deity and Protestants run the other way, both extremes are sadly in error. For the Catholic to make her a god is to miss the raw power of her humanity. For the Protestant to lightly pay her "honorable mention" pitifully misses the dare of God's call to us to become as she was: a bond-slave of the impossible.

Luke 1:37-38 summarizes the conversation between Mary and the angel Gabriel: "[Gabriel said,] *'For nothing will be impossible with God.' And Mary said, 'Behold, the bond-slave of the Lord; be it done to me according to your word.'*" Does that do to you what it does to me? Let's take a moment to unpack this together.

Mary is, at most, 16. There is absolutely no precedent for what she is hearing. The closest thing that might have crossed her mind was that of much older, married women of the Old Testament who were given children of promise…along with their husbands!

Mary is on an island in this category. There is no other way to describe this encounter other than astonishing in its reach and stunning in its ramifications. Yet, something in the transcendence of the moment pushes Mary to the conclusion that she must become a bond-slave to this impossibility! Hear that again; she happily surrendered herself as a *slave* of the Lord and His offer of doing the impossible.

Bill Johnson says it this way: "Our debt to the world is an encounter with God."[2] To that end, we must become bond-slaves of the impossible. A people of a covenant to live beyond our means! To do works that transcend my limited abilities to show the world a God of unlimited abilities.

If all the Church is offering is clean living born out of good doctrine then we have certainly become what Paul warned us about, *"...holding a form of godliness although they have denied its power...avoid such men as these"* (2 Tim. 3:5).

We owe our culture a living, visible demonstration of the Kingdom of another world. Jesus told His disciples to heal the sick and define that moment of healing as the Kingdom's appearance on earth. I'm not batting a thousand on that command, *yet*....

But all around me are the evidences of the Kingdom's Transcendent Supremacy. Just to name a few: A premature baby alive and well. Or a case of vertigo, gone in an instant. A lifetime of back pain smashed by Kingdom Come. Cancer....*gone*. A multiple-year stomach ailment removed overnight. Ten new clients in a budding new ministry for the eradication of addictions...delivered by the power of the Kingdom and a Kingdom warrior named Steve. A marriage dragged back from the abyss into abundant living. Mental illnesses erased. An ocean that could not break my son-in-law's neck. An unbeliever who walks into our gathering and hears the prophetic reading of his heart. Story after story of recent conversions into an irresistible Kingdom that draws humans into an encounter with God not because they were threatened with hell to come but because they tasted Heaven on earth in the Kingdom *now!*

I'm a happy slave of conquering the impossible. I've discovered the true nature of Christianity is the presence of the Kingdom of Heaven on earth. I've heard it said that when we get to Heaven "someday" that we're in for a lot of surprises. While I'm sure that's true, I've decided to take a different path of life that minimizes my surprises tomorrow through discovery *today*.

Just prior to World War II amphibious landings were deemed impossible due to notable failures in World War I. MacArthur, Eisenhower, and other heroes of that day never got their boots wet in basic training for an amphibious assault. A lesser-known military officer, nicknamed "Mad (as in mad-man) Smith" advised the strategists of his day that the war could not be won without large-scale amphibious assaults. "Mad" was told that such an idea was impossible. His answer? "Well, then we are going to do the impossible and we are going to do the impossible WELL." Mr. Mad was a bond-slave to the impossible.

I love the following quote from Bill Johnson:

> I'm not looking to "empty" my mind, I'm looking to *fill* my mind with the thoughts that God carries for me. I can't afford to have a thought in my head about me or my immediate sphere of influence that God does not have in His Head about me or my world. What I cannot afford is to be impressed with the size of a problem, world condition, or my own circumstances. I try to live

in such a way that none of those things are ever bigger in my consciousness than God.[3]

Mad, Mary, Randy, Bill...any more bond-slaves out there?

ENDNOTES

1. Malcolm Gladwell, *The Tipping Point: How Little Things Can Make a Big Difference* (Back Bay Books, 2002).

2. Johnson, *When Heaven Invades Earth*, 133.

3. Bill Johnson, in a recent sermon at Bethel.

Chapter 23

"Look at Us!"

O nce again, Dr. Luke must have felt like he was losing his mind. None of his medical training prepared him for the astonishing events he was called upon to record. In his Gospel he told of how the crushing masses were being overwhelmed with a force field of health and well-being that was flying out from the sheer presence of Jesus. Now, he is recording the Acts (notice, not the doctrine, the standards, or the belief system of, but the *Acts*) of the apostles.

Peter and John are walking time bombs of a Transcendent Supremacy. They are pregnant with the Kingdom of God within them. They've spent days, weeks, maybe months soaking the King's influence into their bodies, souls, and spirits. And as if all that was not enough, the Day of Pentecost took them right over the edge. If they didn't get more outlets soon, somebody was going to get… well, not hurt, but really healed. And then *it* happened.

They are going to the temple at the hour of prayer, not to *get* prayer, but to release the Kingdom in their praying. Interesting, isn't it? We often go to church to "get" prayer, when the truth is, we should be loosing the King's reality *through* prayer everywhere and at all times. What would happen if the next time you went to church, you went to release the pent-up flood of the Kingdom of God within you? What if thousands of us did that the next time we go? I'll tell you what would happen: A lame culture would rise up and walk in the Spirit…but I'm ahead of myself.…

A lame man had been laid daily at the gate called "Beautiful" so that he could beg for money. Humanistic religion is no better than humanistic politics. Throw money at the problem. It won't do them any good in the long run but we will feel better in the short term because we did something, and we get to be seen doing it by everyone passing by. That's not compassion; that's enslavement, for both parties. Am I against helping the poor? Not at all. I do it formally and informally almost every day. All I'm saying is that feeding the hungry can be done by an atheist as easily as a believer.

The believer's dilemma is that we are too easily satisfied with that alone. As I stated earlier, C.S. Lewis once said that the problem with modern Christianity is just that: WE ARE TOO EASILY SATISFIED WITH MODERATE BLESSINGS AND GAINS when richer realities await our faith!

Dr. Luke said that the man looked at Peter and John. Then Peter said something positively and wonderfully redundant: *"Peter…said…'Look at us!'"* (Acts 3:1-10). I believe that in that crack of time, that seam of the eternal breaking in on the temporal, that the man saw a flash of what was coming at him. The insuperable prominence of Christ's influence was coming at him at the speed of light through the hand of Peter who "seized him" by the hand, made him stand and leap and leap and leaping, praising God.

It is time, TODAY, for all of us who believe that the invincibility of the Kingdom of God is within us to SEIZE some hands with more than our material answers, *but with our transcendent goods!* We have the potential of a prominence that could roar out from us. Mountains are supposed to move when we speak. Ten people are supposed to SEIZE US, begging to be taken with us to our God (see Zech. 8:23). Whole nations are supposed to be discipled and, yet, it is not an unbelieving "outside world" that is the problem here…it is unbelieving "believers."

"Look at us!" Indeed….

Within us is the same force field that leveled the fields around Jesus. Within us is the same excellence of a presence that was pulsing through His clothing, beaming out of His words and stampeding the inferior reality of darkness. Within us, behind our eyes, waiting a *moment* when you are too bulgingly pregnant to hold the promise within you anymore.

Push it out and say to someone today, "LOOK AT US!"

I Don't Want to Go to Heaven!

What I *want* is this: I WANT HEAVEN ON EARTH!

If a complete stranger walked up to me in a public place with the intention of creating an artificial "witnessing" encounter I might be tempted to give them a wide berth so I could respond. Here's how that scene might look:

Unsuspecting **W**itness **T**rainee: "Excuse me sir, could I have a minute of your time?" Seeing his clipboard covered with Bible verses I might say,

Me, in a mood: "Sure kid. What are you selling?" (I might even toss a cuss word or two into the mix just for fun.)

U.W.T.: "Oh, I'm not selling anything, sir. In fact, I'm giving a free gift. The gift of salvation. Would you like to know for sure that if you die today, you would go to Heaven?"

Me, in even more of a mood: "Listen, Skip, that is your name right? (He has a name tag…sorry, I forgot to tell you that.) I would really rather live today, if it's all the same to you. (Boy, some cuss words would really spice this up…) And while I'm living, I want Heaven on earth."

Skip (he's the guy with the name tag I forgot to mention): "That's a really nice thought sir…but what I really want to talk to you about is your eternal soul."

Me, with an ever-increasing mood: "Skippy boy, are you aware that the eternal God calls Himself 'I AM'? You see, my eternal soul is living in this one and only moment we are standing in…and right now, all over the world, Skip, hell is owning far too much of this one and only moment. If I am going to Heaven someday, and I am certain that I am, I want to live in this one and only moment of eternity that I know anything about and make sure that the space my sack of bones occupies is being increasingly invaded by the reality of Heaven right here on earth…."

Skip, looking for a way out: "I'm sorry, sir. I didn't mean to bother you…."

Me…the mood…you get the picture: "*Shhhh…I wasn't finished, Skip*. And if I want anybody to go to Heaven with me, I want to be absolutely certain that to begin with I am serving up sufficient doses of Heaven's irresistible inescapability. When complete strangers walk past me, I want them to pause, turn around, and be overwhelmingly inclined to ask me, 'What was that?' or 'Excuse me, sir, when I passed through your shadow my dislocated shoulder popped back into place.' Skip, have you ever prayed the most prayed prayer in history…not the sinner's prayer there on your clipboard…but, 'Our Father, who art in heaven, hallowed be Thy name. Thy kingdom come, Thy will be done on earth as it is in heaven….' You know it, right, Skip?"

Skip nods yes. His eyes appear a bit glazed and his balance is questionable.

Me…the mood turning to a Radiance: "Don't pass out on me just yet, Skip. I'm almost finished. Is there any mention in that prayer about, 'if I die today'? No. It seems to me that the passion of that prayer is for God to sustain my life with enough food and forgiveness that I am a healthy, living portal, a biological bridge and an army of one for Kingdom Come wherever I stand."

Skip is pale, knees buckling, clipboard falling to the ground: "Sir, would you pray for me? I'm feeling a bit light-headed."

Me…vibrating with a Transcendent Supremacy: "Sure, Skip. Father, unload Heaven on this patch of earth. Fill Skip with Heaven. Come…Thy Kingdom Come…*now*…."

Skip rolls into a happy little heap on the ground; his clipboard now pressed up against his face.

I believe that our witness is born in the following Transcending realities: "If you are raised up with Christ, keep seeking the things above, where Christ is seated at the right hand of God."

"Now to Him who is able to do above and beyond all we can ask or think, according to the power that works with in us…."

"Built together into a dwelling of God in the Spirit" and *"grow up in all aspects into Him, who is the Head, even Christ."*

If only these few passages become Transcendent Supremacies within us our witness would be Heaven Air around us.

I WANT HEAVEN ON EARTH! I want to be one gift of the five (apostle, prophet, evangelist, pastor, and teacher) who is equipping the saints with a determination that the goal is nothing less than, *"the measure of the stature which belongs to the fullness of Christ. As a result, we are no longer children, tossed here and there by waves…"*; which coincides with the words of Christ when He promised, *"If you abide in Me and My words abide in you, ask whatever you wish, and it shall be done for you."*

Mountains of a lesser-ranking to the Mountain of the House of God not only move, they are disintegrated by the presence of God in the arrival of Sons and Daughters of Heaven's Substantiality. When we live in the Heavenlies because we are consistently connected to our position of being seated with Him, Heaven arrives in every step we take on earth.

"But, pastor! That's *just* my spiritual life…what about my 'secular' life?"

Heaven on earth means that everything came from God and is going to God, which by implication means that *everything*, and I mean *everything*, is spiritual and *nothing*, and I mean *nothing,* is secular!

When I pray, that's spiritual. When I have lunch with my friends I don't "turn off" spirituality, I bring it into that arena. When I go to church, that's spiritual. When I go to a board of education meeting, that's spiritual. When I sing at church, that's spiritual. When I sing "Wild Thing" in my car, that's spiritual. Do you know what will happen when a sufficient number of us believe and live this to be the most superior reality on earth? Heaven will start arriving on earth in ever-increasing dosages!

I WANT HEAVEN ON EARTH! Hell has been here too long. It's a tired old reality. It's time for hell to go to hell where it belongs. And, it's time for Heaven to COME TO EARTH WHERE IT BELONGS!

I want Heaven on earth; I have ordered my priorities to be one of those in the fanatic fringe of the imbalanced people whose lives are ordered toward all of Heaven's priorities. Everything here ought to be connected to there and it is our life's purpose to bridge that gap.

Heaven aches for a powerful and significant interaction with earth. Every answer to any prayer is that God unloads more and more of the Holy Spirit into our life and space (see Luke 11:13). *We* seek for answers to prayer and God seeks to make us answers to our own prayers by granting us more Holy Spirit.

We seek for God to change things on the earth and God is seeking to empower us to make us History makers on the earth. We seek for God to intervene and God seeks to pour more Holy Spirit on our lives to have boldness to intervene with the supernatural evidence of the Kingdom of Heaven on earth. We seek for God to make things right and God seeks to make *us* right in order to spread righteousness in all the earth. We pray problems; God wants to prophesy solutions through our prayers by the Holy Spirit.

A couple of nights ago I was awakened with a start at 2:45 A.M. My heart was pounding and my mind raced, "What's up, God?" He said, "Everything's fine. You're OK. Go back to sleep." Hmm.

The next day this person shows up at my office whom I have never met or ever heard of and says, "Last night I woke up at 3:00 A.M. and this voice says to me, 'If you go and see Pastor Randy Dean, everything is going to change.'"

I prayed with that person to lead them to Christ and when we opened our eyes, Heaven was in the room. Knock, knock, knocking on Heaven's door is not a bad idea—but the reality is that it is more like, HEAVEN IS KNOCKING ON OUR DOOR!

P.S. Nobody named Skip was actually harmed in the making of this chapter…not yet, anyway.…

Chapter 24

RAISE THE DEAD

Raise the dead....
—Jesus

What is it about Jesus and His claims that can really push our buttons? What is it about His words, like from Matthew 10:8: "*...heal the sick, raise the dead, cleanse the lepers, cast out demons...*" that simply and flat-out can make us uncomfortable?

I can get somewhat comfortable with this if I massage it to say, "Heal sick minds and situations, raise dead hopes, cleanse the people of your day who feel dirty, remove demonic influences." Make no mistake about it, we *are* called to do such things, and I believe in and practice obedience to the same.

The problem we are left with here is that Jesus said this in a far less complex way out of the reality that He was doing these things. Such as...healing *really* sick people, raising *really* dead people, cleansing the *real* lepers, and casting out demons that would visibly enter pigs!

I'm concerned that greater numbers of believers aren't seriously addressing the simplicity of a command that seems to me to be fairly straightforward. To me it is vitally important that we sincerely address a matter like this.

First of all, why should such an outrageous claim by Jesus need to be addressed? Why should we bother to wrestle with His expectation? *Why?* Because, like the mountain to the climber, it is there.

Second, it strikes me that Jesus gave us this order with the full intention of frustrating us. I don't remember who said this, but I am sure glad I was around to hear it: "Frustration is a blessing to the future."

As long as gas was 25 cents a gallon we were happy to drive gas hogs. When it hit a dollar a gallon, frustration set in and we started envisioning the future. But cars of tomorrow will be better yet because we've refused to sidestep the frustration.

Advice we listen to, but pain we obey.

Let's simplify matters and focus the pain of just one of the four challenges that Jesus proposed: Raise the dead. That's all.

Sorry.

What we must remember is that Jesus speaks to us from His own native soil, Heaven's Kingdom. We are the foreigners. His is the native tongue and it is our obligation, if we have any desire at all to function even nominally in the Kingdom of God, to lean into His *lingua franca* and once and for all to learn to speak His language.

"But Pastor Randy! Raise the dead? Even the prospect of discussing the matter is unsettling. Can't we just move along and leave this sort of thing to the occasional 'leading of the Spirit'? Or maybe the experts, like missionaries and big-name personalities. Wouldn't that make more sense?"

Are we terrified that we might learn something that would steal us away from our own agendas? Are we so currently spiritually vibrant and attractive that there is simply no room for any more of God's beauties to be seen in us? Has a watching world around us been swept up in a trembling swoon at the sheer magnitude of the goodness of God at work within us? (See Jeremiah 33:3,9.)

Former associate editor of *Fortune* magazine, cultural and business futurist, Alvin Toffler said, "The illiterate of the 21st century will not be those who cannot read and write, but those who cannot learn, unlearn, and relearn."

Sounds very similar to what the apostle Paul said: "…*always learning and never able to come to the knowledge of the truth.*" We have to jettison our excuses and marginalizing if we ever expect to be filled with enough Life to raise the dead.

What if our need for more conferences and discussions on what needs to change in the Church comes down to something as simple as this one command that Jesus gave us? *Raise the dead.*

I heard a man say once that the most straightforward way to start and build a church would be to raise the dead on day one. Then on the following day, raise the dead. And on the third day, raise the dead. Whatever else you would do would be decoration from that point, because without a doubt, you would have a congregation.

It comes down to this: Jesus' command from the aforementioned reference in Matthew is concluded with, *"...freely you received, freely give."* **Internal splendor can become external health for the benefit of those in need.**

As I observe the generalized "us," the collective bin of believers alive today, I hear the Holy Spirit shouting, "You cannot regain externally what you've lost internally. You cannot restore material systems before you reclaim true spiritual power. You cannot win spiritual domain swinging humanistic weapons. You cannot regain through political clout what you've lost in spiritual clarity. Healing the sick, raising the dead, cleansing the lepers, and casting out demons is irretrievably rooted in freely receiving that you may freely give!

Like baby birds in a nest, learn to receive Heaven's Kingdom with Heaven's King in a saturated certainty throughout all your internal realities. I have a Niagara of Life awaiting channels for release. You have but to unmercifully slay stunted human reasoning and be resurrected to a revolution of *real Life"*

I want to be perfectly clear with you, my readers. I have only done this…raise the dead, that is, one time. I've lost count of the number of times I've tried. The point is, I'll never forget that one time.

A friend and I came upon an accident scene in Austin, Texas. A teenaged girl was crawling out of a creek bed just in front of a bridge railing. She was muddy and bleeding.

We stopped to give her aid. It was obvious that she was in shock and she was crying out something about her friend being under a car in the creek. Standing there with her we saw what she was describing. At one point, this young lady screamed, "Jesus, help me!" I said, "He's right here…in me," and she fell into my arms sobbing.

My friend went to check on the girl under the car. She was almost completely under the car with her hand barely visible just to the side of one of the exterior mirrors. When he checked, she had no pulse. Due to the angle of the car he could see that her head was stuck in the mud with the car roof directly on her right temple. We looked at each other and knew immediately to call for life to return…we did and life suddenly flew into that young lady's mouth. She immediately started sucking air!

Within a few minutes other cars and people came on the scene to help. Before long there were enough of us to lift the car off the girl in the creek. When the ambulance helicopter arrived, she stopped breathing again. The paramedic said, "Don't leave us now, little girl." Again, my friend and I looked at each other and said, "Life, come back!" Instantly, again she sucked air.

Days later when I saw her in the hospital, though we had never actually met, she smiled and said, "You're the man who prayed!"

Death all around us will be challenged and conquered to the degree that we build within us a Transcendent Kingdom of Radiant Life. If Jesus said that the end result would be that we will raise the dead to the extent that we have freely received that kind of Transcending Life, then, my dear readers, we have an opportunity waiting before us.

You cannot give what you do not have. That's not meant to shame or blame; it is meant to motivate us to discover more of that Life until our life has enough surplus to give that Life.

THE VALUE SYSTEM OF HIS SACRIFICE

If my faith is not reaching into the value system of His sacrifice I will end up walking in some kind of sin. Not the kind of sin that robs a liquor store, but the "church-y" sin that allows for a self-righteous bigotry and shame-based vision of God.

Sin is simply and terribly "missing the mark," misfiring at the bull's eye and sending an arrow to a less satisfying but more easily achieved destination.

What we are being called to learn is that the finest format for obedience is based on a heart that yearns to be trained, mentored, transformed, renewed, and fully engaged and nurtured in the environment of a holy holistic Creator. Obedience rooted, for instance, in any of a number of versions of a heavenly Father in need of some kind of anger management due to His ever-shrinking patience with our behavior or a loudly ticking clock in the Throne Room is not obedience, but, in fact, is dysfunctional at best and dreadfully shame-based at worst.

But in the environment of a holy holistic Creator, everyone and everything is getting *healed*.

In the other environment where the pressure is on and "shame on us if we fail," everyone, including the health care givers, is getting more diseased and dying.

We need to get a grip! If I am not raising the dead (or for that matter, healing the sick, casting out demons, and cleansing lepers...sorry, I know I said we would only go after one thing of the four), then I have yet to receive what He is offering to the degree that He is offering it!

Raising the dead is a routine possibility for anyone willing to flood their inner reality with His Radiance! A grip on the True and Living God whose vision for His creation was fully finally secured in the words of His Son on the cross, "IT IS FINISHED!" The Law and the Prophets have been fulfilled, the Kingdom of God is at *your hand*, the Lamb of God has taken away the sin of the world, The

Father has looked at the anguish of His Son's soul and He is satisfied! The magnificent Redemption of Christ Jesus trumps all notions of death, disease, and destruction. So...

Raise the dead!

"ALL THINGS ARE POSSIBLE..." (MARK 9)

In Mark 9:23 Jesus said, *"All things are possible to him who believes...."* This too can be one of those statements that will just sit there, staring at you, daring you to do something with it or just flat out throw it away. No middle ground. Or, I should say, no honest middle ground.

What I mean by honest middle ground is that found in the context of this outrageous statement. The story goes like this: A desperate father brings his demonized son to the disciples for help. We aren't told what they did, just that whatever they did, did nothing. (Sound painfully familiar?)

It is clear that they tried because the man said, *"...they could not do it...."* Another thing that is clear is that the man at first says that he brought his son to Jesus, and then later clarifies that he really brought the boy to the disciples. This isn't a contradiction but rather a striking clarification; when we are impotent, observers will account that to Jesus and that absolutely, positively must *not* be OK with us for it brings dishonor to His fully honorable name.

Jesus underscores this point by sharply rebuking His boys: *"How long shall I put up with you? Bring him to Me!"*

The phrase "put up with" has a meaning akin to fierce restraint, not just an average case of patience. When they bring the boy to Jesus, the demon acts out in convulsive self-destructive violence. Later in the account the father warns that this behavior has thrown the child into fires and water to destroy him.

You know what I mean when I say, "Somebody call 911!"?

Then Jesus does something that we all need to think about: He calmly asks, *How long has this been happening to him?* Watch this carefully now: Jesus, Son of God, able to read thoughts and unlock the secrets of our hearts seems to want information unavailable to Him. Or is there something deeper going on?

Can you see this in your mind's eye? The disciples are toeing the ground, embarrassed and maybe trying to think of something spiritual to say. Like, "It's not about us anyway, right Jesus? We tried, but You must increase, we must decrease. After all, this way You will truly get the credit…right Jesus? Uh, Jesus…shouldn't You hurry up and do something? This is getting messy…Hey, Jesus, do You see the campfire right behind us? Oh yikes! This crowd is getting huge. Tick-tock, Jesus…. Wait a minute…hey Peter…maybe Jesus isn't going to do anything about this. Yea, that's it! Jesus just wants us to know that this is a lifelong struggle for this family."

As the pregnant pause reaches a crowning, painful birthing point, Jesus does not yet push even when the father begs, *"If You can do anything, take pity on us and help us!"* Then, when the tension has reached an unbearable crest, Jesus answers, *"If You can?"*

Now bear with my imagination again as we turn back to the disciples; Jesus might have said, "I don't know...what do you guys think? Can I?" I believe that every second of pause in this discourse is for the sake of driving home a lifelong lesson in the 12.

"All things are possible to him who believes." And while this should be the battle cry of the Church, we have all too often defaulted to the next words; the despondent cry of the father, *"I do believe; help my unbelief."* Please hear me; I have been as given to this as anyone reading this, but I am pleading with you and myself to pull ourselves *upward* for the prize of the call of God in Christ Jesus: *"All things are possible to him who believes."*

Where would you rather live the rest of your life? In the fully understandable despondent cry of the father (I believe; help my unbelief) or in Transcendence of Jesus' command upon the moment, "All things are possible to him who believes"?

The conclusion of this account is that Jesus commands the spirit to leave and in an instant the boy is so still he seems dead. (Side note: some of the crowd must have thought that Jesus killed the kid because of the way Mark records it: *"Most of them said, 'he is dead!'''*) When the disciples finally get some privacy (which I'm sure was none too soon for them) they asked Jesus why they could do nothing. Listen to me: *We need to be asking the same question!*

In an earlier chapter I've queried, "How dare we be powerless?" The world we live in is serving up thousands of opportunities every day for the Kingdom of God to demonstrate the Absolute Goodness of God. But we keep looking for spiritual-sounding words instead of paying heed to the answer Jesus gave 2,000 years ago in this prophetic story: *"This kind cannot come out by anything but prayer."*

And yet, notice, Jesus never prayed over this boy! It is clear, then, that He was not saying that when we really learn how to pray about problems they will leave. He *is* saying that when we learn to be people who live and breathe in prayer, unceasingly, we will have a bank vault full of an intimacy and reality of God that will catapult every dark thing that comes anywhere near our sphere of influence.

The humbling of the 12 in this story is ours too. But the difference is, they didn't have the convenience of the pages I just used to teach the principles of the Kingdom. They had a matter of months to learn what we have had a matter of centuries to absorb. If Jesus felt "fierce restraint" then, what must He feel today?

Here's my passionate cry on His behalf: arise and slay the unbelief holding you back! Every time you hear yourself being the victimized father in this story rather than the fully discipled son or daughter of God you are called to be, do whatever you must do to run to the manifest presence of God and pray. And when you pray, do not pray the problem! Prophesy the solution of the Body of Christ becoming the abiding Temple of the Holy Spirit through prayer…and then…

Chapter 25

ABIDE THERE UNTIL
YOU RADIATE HIM

God Is Spirit (John 4:24).

The Holy Spirit is God. God is the Holy Spirit. As God is Father and God is the Son, so God is Spirit.

Are we walking this earth with that reality beating in our chest? Something in me says that if we did, we Christians would be massively different than we are and the truest character of God would be far more accurately advertised. Something else in me shouts that the Church of today needs an extreme makeover, the likes of which are only possible if God the Spirit does the making over.

Not clever church growth experts who have not paid a bloody price for laying down their lives for a people in the inner city, or as is my case, in the middle of nowhere, an outer city. In their mindset, the classic church growth model today works best in the best of demographics, but so does a retail outlet store. No Spirit required.

The family from our church that I've mentioned throughout this book, who has been in central Mexico for 25 years, recently experienced a dispute over the land surrounding their church. The man behind this dispute was so determined to make his point that he built a fence around the church property to prevent people from getting to the church. Since most people walk to this church, either directly from home or from taxis and buses that drop them off at quite a distance from the church, this man was convinced he had put a stranglehold on the church.

My friend emailed me and said, "Pastor, this has been a real blessing to us! Since the fence went up, more people are coming to church and the Spirit is falling on all of our meetings. They climb over and under that fence. They help each other and do whatever they can to get here in bigger numbers now than before." I wrote him back and I told him that I thought every church ought to have a fence around it. (By the way, the fence is now gone and the Spirit isn't.)

Come, Holy Spirit! Be God Almighty in me and in the church that I pastor. Come ruthlessly to heal every layer of the wreckage of humanity that intrudes in what should be the beauty of the Bride of Christ. Come, Holy Spirit, and fearlessly rebuke satan in every one of us the way Jesus did when Peter was too ignorant to know the difference between the things of God and the things that are just human. Come, Holy Spirit, and tell us that we don't know what spirit we are of when we, like Jesus' own 12 disciples, with judgmental religious thinking were eager to call fire down on "bad people."

Come, Holy Spirit! We repent for making You "God Jr." We repent for making You the author of parlor tricks that only entertain our perverse curiosity. But we also repent for boxing You in, pouring water on Your Fire, telling You how to pray instead of letting You pray the ragged, raw, and real passions of Your needs. Come, Holy Spirit, in nothing less than the full majesty of God in us, to make Jesus Christ more Lord in and through us than He has ever been before.

The Housebroken Gospel

In 1980 I picked up a marvelous Newsletter, "Life Changers" by Bob Mumford. I have no idea how it came to be mine, but today, it is still in my possession. The heading of this section is the title of an article in that Newsletter. Here's a sample of why I treasure it so:

> During the height of the Charismatic explosion several years ago [remember, this was written in 1980], an itinerant, Pentecostal evangelist from Arkansas was ministering throughout South Florida. His sermons always had one theme: What God was doing in the earth today. And no matter what text or outline he followed, almost every sermon included the following story:

"One spring when I was a youngin' growin' up in Arkansas, I found me a baby coon. Its mother had been kilt and it was all alone. I took that little bitty coon home and raised it up like it was a part of the family. I fed him from a bottle, let him sleep in my bed when mama wasn't watchin' and took him rompin' in the woods.

"Come fall when that coon was near full growed, he started actin' peculiar. He had been down to the creek a catchin' crawdaddies and a chasin' miners and one cold night when the moon was full he got to actin' fidgety. Somethin' was a'stirrin' inside of him. He didn't know what it t'was, but catchin' crawdaddies and seein' the full moon was a makin' him remember he was a wild critter. Didn't make no matter I'd raised him up tame; he was borned a wild critter and nothin' could change him. He wanted to be free! He couldn't never be happy a'livin' tame, cause he was wild to the core! It twern't long 'til he lit out for the creek and I never see'd him again.

"Friends," he would continue, "you got to know the Church is a wild critter just like that coon. She was borned free on the day of Pentecost but men has tried to tame her down. They've done put her in buildin's and tried to keep her shut up in all kinda doctrines and theology. But the Church has been down to the creek where she belongs and she ain't been a'catchin' crawdaddies, she a'been gettin' filled with the Holy Ghost! The Spirit of God is arisin' up in God's people and they're doin' the things that should come natural to them. They're a'movin' in the Spirit, speakin' in tongues, prophesyin', and a'healin' the sick, cause the Church has seen the full moon and somethin' is a'makin' her fidgety, cause the Church is a knowin' what she was borned for! Y'all say, 'Amen!' Everyone said, 'Amen!'"

Bob went on to say that this is exactly what has happened to the Gospel of the Kingdom of God since the first century. He said:

"The dynamic and power of the Gospel has been tamed, domesticated and housebroken to the point of bearing little resemblance to the free and powerful Body that was born on the day of Pentecost. 'Taming' is defined as 'reduced from a state of native wildness so as to be useful to man.' 'Domesticate' means 'to adapt to life in intimate association with and to the advantage of man.' And to 'housebreak' is to 'make tractable or polite.'

"Y'all say, 'Amen!'" [1]

Kris Vallotton says something like this, "We've got to stop measuring our churches by how many *come* to church and start measuring them by how many *become* the church." The greatest need of our time is sending people out with

God the Spirit saturating their lifestyles so that when they encounter seekers on the streets, in their workplaces, walking school hallways, or living next door, they are sensitive to the Spirit's strategy for a transcendent moment to introduce the atmosphere of Heaven.

These seekers are everywhere! If they are not coming to our worship gatherings, we need to be reminded of the promise of Zechariah 8:23, which says that ten people will grasp our garment and beg to go with us because they have heard that God is with us!

If He is with me, ten people will be with me too.

So, whether we intersect a genuine seeker sitting next to us on Sunday morning or sitting next to us on an airplane, our goal must be the same; we must be the bearers of God the Spirit and His undeniable force of the immaterial. We must never seek to tame, domesticate, or housebreak Him, for in reality, He is what the seeker intrinsically desires!

In his book, *The Gospel According to Starbucks*, Leonard Sweet tells the story of T.S. Eliot, one of the most influential poets of the 20th century.[2] Eliot liked to tell of a sign outside a baker's shop advertising bread for one dollar a loaf. You go into the shop, he said, hungry for bread and imagining the fresh smell of bread right out of the oven, only to find that inside the shop all that is for sale are copies of the sign advertising bread. Eliot suggested that the Church was too much like that shop.

THE EVIDENCE OF THE BAPTISM
IN THE HOLY SPIRIT

I was taught early on in my Christian experience that the initial physical evidence of the Baptism in the Holy Spirit was speaking in other tongues. I respect that and I have done that. My life today is more healed, more alive, and more fruitful because I have learned to plumb the depths of that gift for my own vitality.

But I no longer believe that gift alone is the irrefutable evidence of the Spirit's Life in me.

Before I go any further I want you to know that I have a grand appreciation for the people who paid a very real price for pioneering the Pentecostal and Charismatic Renewal of the last century. My wife's grandparents were two of those people.

Paul and Naomi Holdridge, or Pappaw and Meemaw, for those who loved them most. Pappaw was a pastor for 50 years in the South and Southwest region of the United States. As a young man he attended Southern Methodist University in Dallas, Texas. But something happened to him on his journey to becoming a Methodist minister.

After being married to his granddaughter for several years and still not knowing what had happened to him I decided to do something novel…ask.

"Pappaw, how did a Methodist boy like you end up on the wrong side of the tracks as a Pentecostal?" I queried.

He grinned his patented Red Skelton imitation and said, "Meemaw and I went to a revival meeting in Dallas to hear a man by the name of Smith Wigglesworth. He laid hands on us and we were baptized in the Spirit."

My mind froze. I said, "Say that again, please." And he did, complete with the Red Skelton grin.

"Uhm….sir…would you please lay your hand on my forehead right now!" I muttered. And he grinned again and said, "All in due time."

Some months later, from his deathbed, this Truest of Patriarchs laid his hands on everyone in the immediate family. When it came my turn, he rolled out of bed, got that Red Skelton grin and blessed me. Transcendence is real… and once again, it is on me while I'm writing these words.

Let me say it again, I have nothing but the highest of regard for the people who paid a price for a treasure we didn't earn but certainly enjoy.

I believe the time has come, however, for another kind of price for the expansive nature of that treasure. Today's treasure does not bury yesterday's, but it most assuredly reaches to the depth of that treasure chest to explore its beauties.

I have come to believe that the truest most quantified and objective manner to know if I am baptized, immersed, drenched, and dripping with the Holy Spirit is Radiance. *The question for today's Spirit-filled believer is this: Is there a measurable Transcendent Supremacy surrounding my life?*

Am I radiant with the unmistakable energy of the Kingdom of Heaven?

If the Church in the Book of Acts spoke in tongues but had no Radiant Sound from Heaven, no crowd would have gathered at their door from the entire region asking, *"What does this mean?"*

(I would dare say that in this context, having ten people clinging to your sleeve each of them clamoring to be heard, shouting at you: "Take us with you! We've heard that God is with you!" is the evidence of the Baptism in the Spirit. How often do we read in the Gospels the pains that Jesus took just to *get away* from those who fought for an opportunity just to touch Him?)

If Peter spoke in tongues but his sermon did not pierce the hearts of the hearers (see Acts 2:37), would we still say he was Spirit-filled? The language of that moment depicts a javelin thrown that ultimately and violently stings its target. His audience cried out in a way that seems to me, stopped the sermon as they pleaded, *"What shall we do?"*

If they spoke in tongues but no wonders (what were they?) and signs (see Acts 2:43) moved the new believers to such a degree that they were selling off their property and possessions, would we still say they were Spirit-filled?

Or if he had picked the lame man up only to drop him back on the ground would we still conclude that he was as full of the Spirit as he ought to be since he spoke in tongues?

If they gathered for praise, spoke in tongues for hours in conferences and meetings but when they spilled out on the streets and their shadows passed over the sick and nothing happened, would we still say they were Spirit-filled?

To make sure you understand my heart, I'm not for one moment suggesting that the miracle in our mouths should be forgotten or relegated as a historic anecdote. I am simply and passionately saying that a new day demands a new level of stewardship. Stay where you are and you will keep what you have, but if you will *invest the beginning, you will harvest the completion.*

Romans 14:17 states that the Kingdom of God is in the Holy Spirit's environment of righteousness, peace, and joy. When the Spirit of God is sought, the full potentiality of the Kingdom is in tow! When the Kingdom is sought, the fullness of the Spirit is required. If you quench one side of this equation or the other you will frustrate the potential of both. *Let's be done with any marginalization of the Spirit or the Transcendence of the Kingdom He longs to deliver!*

Everything I've spread throughout all the pages of this book leads back into this chapter. Nothing is unrelated to this moment of the book. The Transcendent Supremacy of the Kingdom and the force of the immaterial beckon us to arise and shine.

"In times of change, learners inherit the earth, while the learned find themselves beautifully equipped to deal with a world that no longer exists" (Eric Hoffer, American social writer and philosopher, awarded the Presidential Medal of Freedom by President Ronald Reagan).

ENDNOTES

1. Bob Mumford, "Life Changers Newsletter" (Hollywood, Florida, 1980).

2. Sweet, *The Gospel According to Starbucks*.

Chapter 26

July 4th—The Not-So-Distant Future

The following is a parable that prophesies…

In the beauty of a predawn Sunday morning, the pastor of a rural Midwestern American church stands in his front yard enjoying the bird's song, the light humid air, and that first sip of coffee. It is the convergence of a Sunday and the Fourth of July and the atmosphere feels like it. Warm, refreshing, and quiet—with something unusual hanging in the air as well.

That first sip of coffee goes down with some difficulty because his emotions are creating that automatic response we call, "a lump in the throat." God is paying a Visit in the front yard of this pastor's home and his mind and heart are racing to capture the essence of what this Visit is all about.

The only prayer that comes to mind is one of praise and proclamation: "For Thine is the Kingdom and the power and the glory…" rolls back and forth from his heart to his mouth. Is it because the nation by and large is going through the motions of celebrating its birthday with little or no gratitude to the God who gave its birthright?

Is it because the sermons he has been preaching are a trumpet call to his rural congregation to arise and seize the Kingdom of God for the benefit of a nation in desperate need of spiritual renewal? Is it because his heart aches for the emergence of the truest purposes of the Church through the living out of the power and glory of the Kingdom of God?

Yes to all of the above.

God is indeed strangely and wonderfully present beyond any recollection of the pastor. God is walking in the cool of the day with another Adam in this early morning drama. The pastor whispers, "Here am I. Send me."

Was it a literal Voice that echoed back? Is someone else hiding around the corner of the house playing tricks with this shepherd's mind?

"Is this really happening" he wondered out loud, "or do I want it to happen so bad that I'm making it happen?" scrolls through his thoughts.

And then the Voice is raised, not shouting, not angry, not strained in any way but raised nonetheless to passion's pitch. *"Arise, shine; for your light has come, and the glory of the Lord has risen upon you. For behold, darkness will cover the earth, and deep darkness the peoples; but the Lord will rise upon you, and His glory will appear upon you. And nations will come to your light...."*

This fully awake dreamer has fallen to his knees with no regard for the dew soaking into his suit pants. Somewhere the coffee cup is fallen on its side having been placed there unawares in the grass. A shaken, delightful, weeping response pours out with bird-songs surrounding, *"Yes, Lord!* Yes, Lord! Let it be so to Your son, Your servant...this day, Lord...Today! *Today!* Be it done to me according to Your Word."

Songbirds now silent, as deep calls back to deep a holy reply, "Stand now and see the Salvation of Your God!"

Chapter 27

CHEEKS AND MILES TO SPARE

In every insult, we have a choice;
transcend or descend.
—Randy Dean

Matthew 5:38-48 is a mystery passage of epic proportions. Is Jesus suggesting that His followers become perpetual victims incapable of feeling pain? Or, as is His usual mode of instruction, is He pressing us to a transcendent dimension of Kingdom understanding?

In the middle of all the slapping, suing, slandering mess of modern culture, Jesus has called out for a new kind of human race. So determined is He to have this become a reality, He became the Seed planted in the earth for a birth of a Radiant Resurrection Race.

His own trial, torture, and death penalty became this Message: all forms of insult, offense, abuse, mockery, robbery, injustice, malfeasance, maltreatment, malpractice, violation, injury, trauma, and any and all effects of any and all wrongdoing are now subject to transcendence for Kingdom purposes.

New creation is formed for response to God, not reaction to life. The first breath taken by Adam and Eve was response to God. When their eyes flew open their life's initiation was full in the face of God. When the last Adam, Christ, laid in the tomb, the same breath of God passed through solid rock and by the Spirit blasted the same life-giving air into every molecule of Jesus' tortured and dead body. From there forward, everything we hope to be is found in response to Him and His face looking into ours. Quite transcendent, wouldn't you agree?

A revolution has begun; not in clean and pretty church services, but in bloody streets of sacrificial love. This Radiant Revolution crushes the opposition by means of the opposition's own strength. Death, in any and all of its hideous forms.

Resurrection is an insurrection irrepressible in a world of revenge. It shouts that Transcendent Love is the final strategy of the Kingdom of God and the greatest unused power of the Church.

I am bowed to a Transcendent Supremacy. The Kingdom of God is within me and profoundly above me. The Life I've discovered in this other world has transformed every layer of my existence.

The sting of your hand on my cheek will not determine the priorities of my life. It will not determine my "feelings." In fact, it may so ignite me in seeing Jesus standing at the right Hand of God that I may turn the other cheek for more inspiration. A slap potentially leads me beyond myself.

We are created for response to God, not reaction to life.

If I am sued and I live in the Kingdom, I respond to God alone and not in a reaction to the court action. If I am bowed to the Transcendent Supremacy of my King and the law of the land demands an unfair mile out of me, I'll reach into the energy of Heaven and give a second mile out my supernatural resources. If my life is lived with the breathing of My Father giving me vitality and energy then no matter what injustice pukes at my feet, it will fail to distract me from my response to Heaven's Face.

In every insult, we have choice; transcend or descend.

To me, the only way that Jesus' immortal and some-times maddening words in Matthew 5 come to life is when I conclude them, as He did, with, "You are to be perfect as your Father in Heaven is Perfect." He lives ABOVE it all and I have the massive privilege to join Him in living *above* it all, even if blood is dripping off my chin.

Have you ever read John 3? I mean before and beyond verse 16? In verse 13 Jesus said, and this is the RDV (Randy Dean Version); "No one has successfully to date made the journey back and forth into Heaven and back to earth except Me. In fact, as you look at Me now—I'm living in both places at the same time."

That's cool, is what that is. He wants to show us how to live in both places at once. That's really what being born again is all about…being Kingdom "Jumpers."

Remember Deacon Stephen in Acts? As he is on earth, being murdered for his faith, he sees the Perfection of Heaven, with Jesus standing at the right hand of the Father. Folks, this isn't some weird lifestyle exclusively reserved for people who wear bathrobes and sandals. This is supposed to be genuine everyday Christianity. We are people from a radiant source of unlimited power.

We aren't being called to live some meager, white-knuckled "niceness." This is an abundant life with cheeks and miles to spare! *If, and I emphasize, If you live bowed to this Transcendent Supremacy: The Kingdom of God.*

HEADS UP, CHICKENS

There is no escaping it: Jesus said it flat out, *"There-fore, you are to be perfect, as your heavenly Father is perfect"* (Matt. 5:48). While you would like to think that a statement that straightforward is pretty hard to dodge, the fact is that most of us have and do. I've sat through more than a few explanations that labored to dumb this down and most of them have left me with the sense that I just have to try harder to be a good boy.

That's not at all what Jesus is getting at. Our Father in Heaven is not a dysfunctional Daddy screaming at us from the sidelines of the game to run faster so He can feel better about Himself. What Hc's doing is inviting us to join Him in heavenly places and to live from the prophetic "amen" He enjoys.

As we have seen, leading up to Jesus' dare to be perfect, He listed a variety of human conditions which, when left to our own resources, we know how to navigate. You punch me; I punch you. You hate me; I hate you. You mistreat me; I mistreat you. Then when the wind is blowing the ashes of our fighting fire with fire, we cry and ask God to fix the mess. In a sense, He is asking us, "How's that working for you?"

But His answer is not to turn us in on ourselves. That's the problem to start with anyway! He dares us to Transcend ourselves and to be risen to heavenly places. He is calling us to live from the perfection of the Father's Kingdom of Heaven.

Perfect here means to live in and see and know the prophetic conclusion of a matter. To experience the "amen" and the "I AM."

God is right now living in His Kingdom of Absolute Perfection. The Prophetic Conclusion is already giving Him massive delight. He lives in that quality and He would like for us to join Him. To live any other way is to live out of the scraps of our own resources.

This is why we should not pray the problems but prophesy the solutions. This is why He taught us to pray, "THY Kingdom COME, THY WILL be DONE on earth, AS IT IS IN HEAVEN." We pray from Heaven *to* earth so that our view is *perfect*. Otherwise we are telling God about how we've been lied on, cheated on, beat on, hated on, country songed on, bluesed on, hip-hopped on, and just generally rocked on by bad people.

I don't know how to say this any other way, so I'll say it in the full context of Matthew 5:38-48 and the words of Jesus: do you just want to cry and feel bad about your real and imagined injustices or would you like to Transcend them all? Would you like to live the highest quality of life available to humankind and delight yourself in a banquet table set in the presence of your enemies? And by the way, God is at the Head of this table.

LIKE CHICKENS WITH THEIR HEADS ON

My seventh grade literature teacher, Miss Ross, made me memorize Rudyard Kipling's poem, "If" and I fumed. Like most seventh graders I had no clue what this stupid assignment had to do with "real life." The opening line says, "If you can keep your head when all about you are losing theirs and blaming it on you...."

I love this poem now. It only took 40 years of real life to learn to appreciate it.

Jesus gave an unblinking, outrageous charge when He said, *"Therefore, you are to be perfect, as your heavenly Father is perfect."* Here's my less-sophisticated version, "Hey, all you chickens in the barnyard! How's this running around like chickens with your heads cut off working for you? Try this; while the axe is swinging, you be the chicken who keeps his head *on*. You'll stand head and shoulders above the crowd."

When we read Matthew 5:38-48 with some serious reflection and meditation we see that Jesus is shouting into the empty cavern of Jewish religious hard-heartedness that longs to give Rome some lessons on morality. Are we any different now? Instead of the empty cavern of Jewish hard-heartedness now it's the empty cavern of Church hard-heartedness that wants to teach America some lessons on morality, even if it kills us…and it is.

Jesus came to lead the world into the greatest Spiritual Revolution and its potential is so vast, deep, and wide that it still has not reached its possibilities. How vast? *Perfection is its only standard.* And not just any perfection, but Heavenly Perfection. Not the perfection we are vainly waiting to be granted *in* Heaven when we get there, but a nitty gritty, punch me in the face on earth and you'll get a blast of Heaven's perfect Father living in me.

Alanis Morissette wrote the song "Perfect" some years ago that throws some light on what we are normally used to when we think of being perfect: "Be a good boy, try a little harder. You've got to measure up and make me prouder…

be a good girl, you've gotta try a little harder. That simply wasn't good enough to make us proud. I'll live through you. I'll make you what I never was...."

We must understand that our Father's perfection is not this version of human dysfunction. His perfection is the substance of His Heavenly Kingdom Life and the quality of His Transcendent Supremacy which He longs to generously pour into us when we decide that "trying harder to be good boys and girls" is vain at best, and self-righteous at worst!

The Greek word for perfect is *teleios,* and it means completeness, the conclusion of an act or state of being, the end prophetic result. God lives in His own conclusions, He is in a constant state of the prophetic *Amen.* There are no loose ends, no unresolved conflicts, no injustices left to right, no matters left for discussion, no unanswered questions, no incomplete statements, nothing left hanging "out there," nothing to discuss and nothing unfinished...HE LIVES IN THAT HIGH LEVEL OF THE QUALITY OF HIS OWN LIFE...where do we live?

Jesus did not write a new law to be performed in a dead state of religious routine. He is baiting humanity out of a lowlife existence dependent on our own discipline to be "good" and into a Transcendence of The Life, radically immersed in Heaven's irreplaceable energy and Love. In fact, in Matthew 5:45 He says this is the only path to becoming the sons and daughters of God.

When the Book of Ephesians says that we are seated in Heavenly Places in Christ, it is not an invitation to "feel" good about the symbolism of being "saved." It's a transcending reality for the believer to be "other" than the other chickens running around the barnyard separated from their heads!

God's Perfection is The Quality of His Kingdom being offered for those who hunger for Life that looks, smells, talks, walks, and *is* the Life of Jesus Christ invested, *for real*, in us.

Smash me in the face and the Life of the Spirit pours out of me and the blood on your knuckles is God's blood. Sue me, curse me, use me under false pretenses and God gets bigger through me. Hate me and the Love of God grows in me and through me.

This is the Revolution of Jesus and this is the hour for the world to see the true face of God in sons and daughters of the Revolution.

Chapter 28

"KINGDOM NOW!?"—THE CRITICS

I chose "Kingdom Now!?" as the title of this final chapter as a reminder that much of what I believe and taught here was dismissed by critics over 20 years ago who labeled such heresy as "Kingdom Now."

Well folks, some of us are still here because the revelation we have tasted and tested is magnificent and true. My son-in-law, Darren Hose says, "Once you truly know something, you cannot un-know it."

In order to adequately wrap up the thoughts and reflections of this book, I would like to review what we've explored with a few new ideas thrown into the mix and yet another perspective from the Gospels.

Our goal, our command, our mission is nothing less than the Kingdom of Heaven explosively expressed, demonstrated, witnessed, and enjoyed on the earth. We are not here to provide the Church as a hiding place from the world. *It is a sin to seek refuge from a storm over which we have been given authority.*

We are here to equip and ignite the Church as platoons of infiltration, saturation, and permeation throughout all of society for nothing less than the eventual healing of the nations through the triumphant resurrection power of the Lord Jesus Christ.

The Kingdom of God is the energy, dynamism, vitality, force, vortex, and potency of Christ's resurrection and ascension to the Right Hand of God's overwhelming competence. It arrives within us, one by one, as a seed when we confess with our mouths and believe in our hearts that Jesus Christ is Lord and that God raised Him from the dead. But, now that seed must germinate.

It must break the surface of the soil and jump up toward the heavens. Food must be found in the fullness of the fruit! (See Mark 4:26-32.)

Saved? Yes, "saved" in that we are made whole from the lost place of Adam's fall and now seated with Christ in the transcendent place of Heaven's destiny to fill the earth. (See Romans 5:15-17; 10:8-10; and Ephesians 2:6.)

The nature of the Kingdom is prominence. It does not come to share a space. It comes to pervasively take over whatever ground it touches. Its nature is to be so prominent that, *"Every knee shall bow and every tongue confess that Jesus Christ is Lord, to the glory of the Father."* This is its character; this is its prowess.

The Kingdom of God is a Transcendent Superiority. It knows no other way to *be* but superior to all other realities. The King is already seated in His exalted Throne. Let every other posing dominion be bound from ill effect or affect. And, let every benefit of Christ's Kingdom be loosed!

It is the nature of the Kingdom to enforce the position of Christ in Heavenly Places on the earth through the joint heirs of Christ, the Body of Christ, the Church. (Read the whole Book of Ephesians!)

What limits would you impose? What boundaries would you draw? There are no toxic limits, no overdose potential.

Micah 4 dares us to believe that the Transcendent Supremacy of the Kingdom's influence has the inherent ability to drive fear and insecurity off the planet to such a degree that all nations will convert their industries of self-defense into agricultural enterprise. And, *that* Kingdom is in our hands! Some have taught us that this possibility only exists at the return of Christ and yet, Micah says that the people groups of the entire world will come "streaming" to *us*!

In that regard, exaltation of self *and* playing small will not serve God honorably. Be done with self-exalting behavior as well as false humility.

The efficacy of the King and His Kingdom is unlimited in scope and scale. If the end of all things is His Kingdom, then the present must, inch by inch and mile by mile, become an adequate witness and demonstration of just how excellent and remarkable that "end" will be.

If its full measure will heal the geopolitical super-structure, shouldn't we be endeavoring to impart it, at whatever level we possess, into any and every smaller fear, insecurity, sickness, and disease if for no other reason than rehearsal? One of the baseline principles of the Kingdom of God is to be faithful over a little which leads to ruling over much.

My passion is to ignite you in every turn of the page with the flames of another world so that when you put this book down its influence will have you smoldering to over-come the lesser realities of the world you will walk through each and every day.

The call inherent to the Kingdom of God is to "sell all" and be relieved of all other competitors for your affections. Indeed, unless you completely buy into the King-dom of God, you will be driven and tossed about by your double-mindedness. *"O taste and see that the Lord is good"* (Ps. 34:8) is a dare to be drawn into the irresistible flavor of God's Transcendent Reality.

It has been said that America's last and best hope is re-vival. While I am sympathetic to the notion, and on many levels cooperative with the concept, it is my personal be-lief that Jesus proclaimed an even greater and more supe-rior transcendence through His delivery of the very real and raw power appearance of the Kingdom of God on the earth. Upon launching His ministry He unapologetically proclaimed that everything from Him forward had the intrinsic potential of being transformed into outrageously good news.

Without so much as a hint of marginalization, He shouted, *"The time is fulfilled, and the kingdom of God is at hand; repent and believe in the gospel"* (Mark 1:15).

Here's that RDV (Randy Dean Version) again: "The wait is over. God has drawn a dark line in the eternal sand. God's total dominion expressed through human beings is presently fully available and simply at the disposal of your own hand. God is far better, bigger, presently available, and massively more potent than you think, so change the way you think. Everything from here forward can be shockingly and fundamentally radicalized into good news."

And then, as if to offer a sample of the raw power and simplicity of His "revival," Jesus journeys to the Sea of Galilee, sees Simon and his brother Andrew doing their work, steps into their space and seizes control of the atmosphere around them. (If it bothers you to think that Jesus' words could "seize control," then think of it another way. Imagine that you have gone all day long without eating anything. As you walk down a city street you pass a restaurant with the aroma of your favorite food positively billowing onto the sidewalk. Let's face it, you've been seized!)

Without a word of explanation other than the unadorned announcement, *"Follow Me, and I will make you become fishers of men. And they immediately left their nets and followed Him*" (Mark 1:17-18).

Herein, Jesus straight away demonstrates the ascendancy of His domain. Again, please allow me the indulgence of a paraphrase: "Hello, fishermen. You are clearly familiar with the tactile pleasure of fish weighing in against your nets as an immediate reward for your craft and knowledge of placing those nets in strategic places and proportions so that the fish don't know they've been caught until it is too late. Their instincts are no match for your clever ability to make a living at the expense of their self-indulgent swimming freedom. Hey, here's a thought. Follow Me, and I will make you fishers of humans."

Upon hearing these words somewhere more deeply than they had ever heard a word in their lives, their hands obeyed a signal from a different source than merely the brain and they dropped their nets in order to make room to grab the insuperable domain, which, quite honestly had already grabbed them.

To further underline these remarkable events Jesus takes His new human catch to the synagogue and teaches. As He speaks, authoritative dominion power (with real effect being put into the atmosphere) is being released in His words (see Mark 1:22). Suddenly, a man with an unclean spirit cries out *the reality of what was happening in the spirit realm!* (See Mark 1:24.) But Jesus would rather speak for Himself, thank you very much. So, He did and cleaned that man's "house" in front of the entire synagogue.

If you continue to follow Mark's account you read with utter amazement at the sheer power of the raw appearance of the Kingdom of God in, around, and through Jesus. Two different homes are physically overrun by the crowds. One of those homes has its roof torn open in order to lower a lame man.

In one place Mark says, *"The whole city had gathered at the door."* In another place Jesus' new "catch of the day" disciples searched everywhere to find Him (because He was out banking into Himself more of the presence of God and the Kingdom) and when they found Him they excitedly kept telling Him, *"Everyone is looking for You"* (Mark 1:37).

So what's my point? Our goal, our command, our mission is nothing less than the Kingdom of Heaven explosively expressed, demonstrated, witnessed, and enjoyed on the earth. We are not here to provide the Church as a hiding place from the world. Again, and for clarity, we must know that it is a sin to seek refuge from a storm over which we have been given authority.

We are here to equip and ignite the Church as platoons of infiltration, saturation, and permeation throughout all of society for nothing less than the eventual healing of the nations through the triumphant resurrection power of the Lord Jesus Christ.

I pray that my passion to ignite you with the flames of another world has done exactly that. What you do when you put this book down can become like a seed planted. Before the idea cools off, do something, anything…now. If you make a mistake, at least make a bold one.

I love the character described by Bob Mumford in chapter 25. Can you hear his Andy Griffith voice cheerfully shouting, "…the Church has seen the full moon and somethin' is a'makin' her fidgety, cause the Church is knowin' what she was borned for! Y'all say, 'Amen!'"

Thank you for giving me the honor of your time and energy to read this book. May His Radiance dominate your every thought and may the core value of every prayer you pray from this day forward be…

KINGDOM… COME… NOW!

ABOUT RANDY DEAN

Living Word Chapel: www.lwc1.com

Randy Dean Ministries:
www.lwc1.com/RandyDeanMinistries.htm

Blog: randydeanministries.blogspot.com

IN THE RIGHT HANDS, THIS BOOK WILL CHANGE LIVES!

Most of the people who need this message will not be looking for this book. To change their lives, you need to put a copy of this book in their hands.

> *But others (seeds) fell into good ground, and brought forth fruit, some a hundred-fold, some sixty-fold, some thirty-fold* (Matthew 13:8).

Our ministry is constantly seeking methods to find the good ground, the people who need this anointed message to change their lives. Will you help us reach these people?

> *Remember this—a farmer who plants only a few seeds will get a small crop. But the one who plants generously will get a generous crop* (2 Corinthians 9:6).

EXTEND THIS MINISTRY BY SOWING
3 BOOKS, 5 BOOKS, 10 BOOKS, **OR MORE TODAY,**
AND BECOME A LIFE CHANGER!

Thank you,

Don Nori Sr., Publisher
Destiny Image
Since 1982

DESTINY IMAGE PUBLISHERS, INC.

*"Speaking to the Purposes of God for This Generation
and for the Generations to Come."*

VISIT OUR NEW SITE HOME AT
WWW.DESTINYIMAGE.COM

FREE SUBSCRIPTION TO DI NEWSLETTER

Receive free unpublished articles by top DI authors, exclusive

discounts, and free downloads from our best and newest books.

Visit www.destinyimage.com to subscribe.

Write to: Destiny Image
              P.O. Box 310
              Shippensburg, PA 17257-0310

Call: 1-800-722-6774

Email: orders@destinyimage.com

For a complete list of our titles or to place an order
online, visit www.destinyimage.com.

FIND US ON FACEBOOK OR FOLLOW US ON TWITTER.

www.facebook.com/destinyimage   facebook
www.twitter.com/destinyimage   twitter